ECOLOGICAL SPIRITUALITY

Ecology and Justice

An Orbis Series on Integral Ecology

Advisory Board Members
Mary Evelyn Tucker
John A. Grim
Leonardo Boff
Sean McDonagh

The Orbis Series on Integral Ecology publishes books seeking to integrate an understanding of Earth's interconnected life systems with sustainable social, political, and economic systems that enhance the Earth community. Books in the series concentrate on ways to:

- reexamine human-Earth relations in light of contemporary cosmological and ecological science
- develop visions of common life marked by ecological integrity and social justice
- expand on the work of those exploring such fields as integral ecology, climate justice, Earth law, ecofeminism, and animal protection
- promote inclusive participatory strategies that enhance the struggle of Earth's poor and oppressed for ecological justice
- deepen appreciation for dialogue within and among religious traditions on issues of ecology and justice
- encourage spiritual discipline, social engagement, and the transformation of religion and society toward these ends

Viewing the present moment as a time for fresh creativity and inspired by the encyclical *Laudato Si'*, the series seeks authors who speak to ecojustice concerns and who bring into this dialogue perspectives from the Christian communities, from the world's religions, from secular and scientific circles, or from new paradigms of thought and action.

Ecology & Justice Series

ECOLOGICAL SPIRITUALITY

Diarmuid O'Murchu, MSC

ORBIS BOOKS
Maryknoll, New York 10545

Manuscript editing and typesetting by Joan Weber Laflamme.

Library of Congress Cataloging-in-Publication Data

Names: O'Murchuu, Diarmuid, author.
Title: Ecological spirituality / Diarmuid O'Murchu.
Description: Maryknoll, NY : Orbis Books, [2024] | Series: Ecology and
    justice | Includes bibliographical references and index. | Summary:
    "An earth-focused spirituality is developed for the ecological needs
    of the Twenty-first century"— Provided by publisher.
Identifiers: LCCN 2023040750 (print) | LCCN 2023040751 (ebook) |
    ISBN 9781626985698 (trade paperback) | ISBN 9798888660256 (epub)
Subjects: LCSH: Ecology—Religious aspects. | Environmental responsibility—Religious aspects. | Human Ecology—Religious aspects.
Classification: LCC BL65.E36 E357 2024 (print) | LCC BL65.E36
    (ebook) | DDC 201/.77—dc23/eng/20231026
LC record available at https://lccn.loc.gov/2023040750
LC ebook record available at https://lccn.loc.gov/2023040751

Contents

Introduction

Drastic weather conditions around the world are changing our human consciousness almost on a daily basis. Just ten years ago, some governments were in utter denial of global warming. Although some still quibble on what our human response should be, this is no longer the case.

Religions and churches are also beginning to wake up, realizing that a moral voice is needed if we are to address this crisis in a more comprehensive way. The desired changes in human behavior are unlikely to transpire without some kind of a spiritual revolution, a new vision emerging in recent decades under the rubric of eco-spirituality.

This new vision is the challenge being addressed in the present work. It is revolutionary in the sense that it invites us to move beyond earlier understandings of spirituality that focus mainly on human holiness and salvation in a world beyond, to a rediscovery of the sacred here on earth, an ecologically focused spirituality propelled at this time by the critical issues facing the well-being of creation at large.

We are invited to reclaim a long lost sense of our identity as earthlings with a divine destiny, not one of escape from this vale of tears but of deeper engagement with the creative Spirit of God forever at work in the evolutionary unfolding of creation itself. This enlarged horizon of faith is still quite new even for the mainline world religions. And the challenges involved in appropriating it for our time are explored throughout the pages of this book.

In conjunction with my previous writings, I wish to call forth a more resilient adult faith in this reappropriation of eco-spirituality. To that end, I wish to provide the adult faith-seeker with material for deeper reflection, leading to a more discerning mode of engagement with the emerging spiritual challenges of the twenty-first century. I, therefore, conclude each chapter with some critical issues for ongoing discernment. Hopefully, these highlighted issues will also serve as material for personal reflection and group dialogue, thus helping to raise the level of consciousness around so many critical issues for faith and religion in the twenty-first century.

1

Eco-Spirituality:
Entering a New Landscape

*And so our lives are spent quietly haunted by the
truth of a connection to nature we can barely admit. In our dream of uniqueness, we forever dance
on the hot coals of a landscape that disquiets us.*
—MELANIE CHALLENGER

*The song is the expression of the moment as it
unfolds, our soul riding the current of the spirits
whose perpetual motion is our becoming.*
—EMMA RESTALL ORR

Two key words constitute the title of this book, *ecological*
and *spirituality*, sometimes combined as *eco-spirituality*.
Of the two, the former is likely to catch the eye and evoke
an internal response, either emotional, spiritual, or both.
Why? It may incite pause because so many major challenges
confront us today in terms of the integrity, health, and
future of our planet, including our own survival, with so
many ecological and environmental crises impinging upon
us—the climate emergency being at the fore in recent times.

Spirituality is a word that excites some, baffles others, and can be downright confusing for those desiring its precise meaning (see Bregman 2014). For many people it denotes a religious perspective, something that follows when we take religion seriously. Since the 1960s it has signified something more than religion can deliver, and, at one extreme, denotes the transcendence (or abandonment) of religion entirely. It also seems to appeal to people who have not inherited a religious upbringing but desire a sense of transcendence in how they engage the world—something bigger and deeper than the experience of ordinary life.

Despite an enormous amount of writing and research on the subject[1]—much of which will be referenced in the present work—spirituality is still a topic requiring a great deal of analysis and, in more religious terms, *discernment*. What is the Spirit of God doing in and through this spiritual awakening? This is an apt question for this project. The landscape becomes all the more challenging when we prefix *spiritual* with the adjective, *ecological*.

Because of the precarious plight of our planet at this time, highlighted, on the one hand, by a range of public media and, on the other, by rigorous scientific research (although not always in agreement), it is easier to clarify what is at stake in the term *ecological* than in the more complex issue of spirituality. Consequently, before elaborating on the ecological dimensions, I devote the opening chapter

---

[1] I first addressed this subject in my 1997 book, *Reclaiming Spirituality*. Much of the same material is reviewed by the British theologian Mary Grey, indicating the shifting nature of spirituality as understood in the closing decades of the twentieth century (Grey 2006). For a more updated assessment, see Lucy Bregman (2014). Sam Mickey (2020) provides an introductory overview of how the ecological dimension entered our understanding of spirituality.

of this book to an overview of spirituality, particularly its evolutionary trajectory since the mid-twentieth century.

Working Definitions

I offer a range of definitions from contemporary writers, but I build around what, initially, looks like an oversimplistic description: *Spirituality is about Spirit connecting with spirit* (note the large S and the small one). I borrow this sense of spirituality from some traditions of Indigenous People around the world (see O'Murchu 2011), and I explore its deeper meaning in later chapters. Foundationally, the simple definition indicates a deep interconnectedness between transcendent Spirit-power (not necessarily God, in the classical theistic sense) and its energetic influence on every living organism, human and nonhuman alike.

By emphasizing connection between Spirit and spirit, this working definition eschews many dualisms that are found in different religious traditions: sacred vs. secular, spirit vs. matter, body vs. soul. Something of that *oneness* that many mystical traditions cherish becomes immediately transparent. Furthermore, this definition reveals the need to link spirituality with the material world we inhabit, including the major environmental challenges facing humanity today.

This book outlines in clearer relief an understanding of spirituality that has been emerging since the cultural uprisings of the 1960s. Drawing mainly on the overview of the French scholar Aurélie Choné (2017, 38–46), eco-spirituality emerged as an organized discourse around the 1980s in the context of a crisis of the environmental movement as well as an interface with diverse religious traditions. Eco-spirituality had been in the making for a long time, and its origins can be traced to Spinoza's pantheistic philosophy in the second half of the seventeenth century and to American visionaries like Henry David Thoreau and George Perkins in the nineteenth century. In the early twentieth century, figures like Rudolf Steiner, the founder of anthroposophy and the father of biodynamic agriculture, along with the Swiss psychologist Carl Gustav Jung and the eco-philosopher David Abram, evoked religious sentiments, advocating links between nature and the human psyche. Among these pioneering figures, none was more outstanding than the priest-paleontologist Pierre Teilhard de Chardin (d. 1955), whose synthesis between faith and evolution brought eco-spirituality into its heyday in the 1970s and for long thereafter.

The Gaia Hypothesis, propounded in the 1970s by the British atmospheric scientist James Lovelock, along with the deep ecology movement pioneered by the Norwegian philosopher Arne Naess, and the ethics for the technological age promoted by German philosopher Hans Jonas, added further depth to the emerging synthesis. Another American movement known as *ecotheology*—represented among others by Catholic priest Thomas Berry (d. 2009), activist Tom Hayden, and ecumenical Protestant bishop Peter Kreitler, sought to bring theology itself into the emerging synthesis.[2] This theological integration was carried forward into the multi-faith realm by the outstanding work of Mary

---

[2] Meanwhile, religious environmentalism was another development forging a further connection between religion/spirituality and ecology. Some of the outstanding names are David Suzuki, Joanna Macy, Steven C. Rockefeller, Roger S. Gottleb, and Bron Taylor. Liberation theology began to move in the ecological direction mainly under the initiative of Brazilian theologian Leonardo Boff. On the wider world religious front was the engaged Buddhism of the Dalai Lama and Thich Nhat Hanh, and the Sufi wisdom of the teacher Llewellyn Vaughan-Lee.

Evelyn Tucker and John Grim of the Center for the Study of World Religions at Harvard Divinity School. From their pioneering work the Parliament of World Religions has hosted several conferences; particularly noteworthy was the 2015 gathering in which the parliament created the Declaration on Climate Change, bringing together more than ten thousand activists, professors, clergy, and global leaders from seventy-three countries and from five major world religions.

Another overview is the feminist contribution of *ecofeminism*. The term *ecofeminism* was first coined in 1974 by the French writer Françoise d'Eaubonne in her book *Le Féminisme ou la Mort*, naming the connection between the patriarchal subjugation of women and the destruction of nature. In it, she argues that women have different ways of seeing and relating to the world than men. These differences can give rise to alternative insights on interactions between humans and the natural world when women's perspectives are considered and brought to the fore within a spiritual context.

Although often cited as an American development with names like Greta Gaard, Susan Griffin, Charlene Spretnak, Carolyn Merchant, Elizabeth Johnson, and most notably Rosemary Radford Ruether, ecofeminism is an international movement, spanning all five continents. Key people in the movement include Ivone Gebara and Vanessa Lemgruber of Brazil, Sallie McFague and Heather Eaton of Canada, the anti-globalization activist Vandana Shiva of India, Val Plumwood and Ariel Salleh of Australia, Mary Mellor and Maria Mies from Europe, and, among African women, Wangari Muta Maathai of Kenya merits special mention. This brief and condensed overview is neatly summarized by the French scholar Aurélie Choné:

The concept of eco-spirituality thus refers to a wide range of discourses, whose common interest is in showing that the current ecological crisis is an essentially spiritual crisis of values, so that answers to it should not be merely technological or material but should be sought on a spiritual level, through the foundation of an "inner ecology" and an enlightened reflection about the meaning of life, the Other, the sacred. (Choné, Hajak, and Hamman 2017, 46)

What More Can Be Said?

My brief overview in itself provides several of the key elements that characterize the landscape I am naming as eco-spirituality. However, very few researchers have taken all those features and woven them into a unified synthesis that could be employed in our time to guide and support those engaged in the discerning task of what is an authentic spirituality for the twenty-first century. Some might rightly suggest that this is an overly ambitious task and not in keeping with the postmodern consciousness of this time, which is not congenial to anything resembling a grand narrative. Others might argue that I am pursuing a vision that will tidy everything up in a field that, of its nature, is complex and characterized by the changes that are endemic to our evolutionary universe.

I have set out to write this book on the conviction that there are features of the contemporary spiritual landscape that have either been ignored in the past or have not been dealt with in an authentically discerning way. Until those items are explored and clarified, the depth and inspiration of eco-spirituality will elude both the practitioners and those seeking to discern its deeper meaning. The following, therefore, are what I consider to be critical issues for any future text on eco-spirituality and, indeed, core dimensions of any authentic spirituality for our time.

1. Eco-spirituality is not necessarily bound to any single religious tradition or family of religious traditions. While wisdom from the religions can enrich our analysis (as highlighted by MacGregor 2018), religious resources can also be major barriers to the deeper and larger landscape that needs to be explored.

2. The dualistic splits between sacred and secular, spirit and matter, continue to haunt the religious imaginations of our world and our human consciousness, preventing us from engaging the enlarged horizon of eco-spirituality.

3. Anthropologies—understandings of the human—that have been largely inherited from classical Greek philosophy and reflected particularly in monotheistic religions like Christianity and Islam are too narrow and reductive for engagement with eco-spirituality. We need to engage an anthropology that honors our true, God-given story of *seven million years*, and not one confined to the past few thousand years.

4. Our theological, patriarchal assumptions also need to be subjected to a more discerning critique, particularly the priority of the male creator God over the energizing Spirit. Chapter 3 engages this claim in detail.

5. The enlarged worldview from modern Western sciences—particularly cosmology, quantum science, and evolutionary unfolding—requires us to revisit the sense of oneness named by mystics down through

the ages, enriching the potential of eco-spirituality as a world-transforming resource.

6. As we transcend former religion-based understandings of spirituality, we will need to adjust to our world of multidisciplinary wisdom, learning to work collaboratively and creatively with a more expansive horizon of wisdom and discernment.

In seeking to honor these expanded horizons and their further elaboration throughout this book, I view spirituality as a consciousness belonging to deep time, predating formal religions by several thousand years.[3] I will also make the bolder claim that this ancient spiritual consciousness espoused a more integrated view of life, often transcending the dualistic separation that continues to haunt the religious consciousness of the modern world. With this more integrated approach, the adjectival prefix *ecological* becomes somewhat redundant, because historically it seems that ancient spirituality was deeply integrated with ecological and environmental concerns.

What did that integration feel like? We get a valuable insight from Karen Armstrong's description of the shaman (the ancient spiritual guide) in prehistoric times:

> The shaman had no conception of what we call the supernatural. He was not looking beyond or above nature, nor was he seeking the divine within himself, like a modern contemplative. Instead, the shaman

---

[3] *Deep time* is a term usually used in geology and astronomy to describe the immense arc of pre-human history. In the study of human origins it is used to describe our sense of time prior to our existence as hunter-gatherers, in other words, before the Agricultural Revolution of some twelve-thousand years ago.

projects his awareness outwards into the depths of the landscape, which for him is alive, spiritually, psychologically and sensuously. He experiences an awareness which he and his community have in common with the animals, insects, and plants around them—even the lichen growing on a stone. Where tribal people sense reciprocity between themselves and the natural environment, we moderns see it as a mere backdrop to human affairs. (Armstrong 2022, 7)

The growing frequency with which ecology features today in both theology and spirituality suggests that an earlier sense of integration somehow got lost or was suppressed in more recent times and is now evoking a fresh awakening whereby the word needs to be rehabilitated anew. And that rehabilitation is prompted by contemporary urgent issues such as global warming, the threat to biodiversity, overpopulation, pollution, ocean acidification, and deforestation.

At the more personal level, I will also address the growing sense of *eco-anxiety* in our time. This relatively new concept is reviewed by Vakoch and Mickey (2022) and is often defined as a chronic worry, distress, or fear concerning ecological devastation; a generalized sense that the ecological foundations of our existence are in the process of collapse. Struggles with eco-anxiety have increased in recent years, and they have been exacerbated by the conditions of the coronavirus pandemic.

As we review this unique spiritual emergence, with both ancient and modern features, we revisit a recurring claim of recent decades: *I am spiritual but not religious*! This is just one of the personal and interpersonal implications of the changing spiritual landscape today. There follows a range of concerns around the meaning of religion in our time (reviewed by MacGregor 2018), alliance with formal religious institutions such as churches, and various attempts at recreating spiritual structures to channel the concerns and aspirations of these emerging devotees.

It is my hope that the reflections of this book will clarify the complex evolutionary nature of eco-spirituality, activating and reinforcing the multiple dialogues that need to happen to translate into practical action a spiritual consciousness that will make life on this earth more enriching and meaningful for humans and non-humans alike.

The Love That Transcends Conditions

Spirituality has long been associated with the flawed nature of the human condition, the life-changes people need to make to become more acceptable to God, and better preparation for eternal happiness in a life to come. A spiritual life was deemed to be a necessary resource to keep on the right side of God so that God would judge us benevolently and bring us home from this vale of tears to where our souls can safely be at rest and enjoy eternal life forever.

Here, we encounter a religion of fear, engaging a distant God that must be pacified and placated through penance and prayer. Such a God is a caricature, a fabrication of our inherited patriarchal culture that seeks to dominate and control, often using the emotional tactics of unworthiness and fear. This is not the God we encounter in the Christian narrative, with Jesus as the human face of God made radically visible on earth, nor is it the God of the Great Spirit described in Chapter 3 below.

Let me once more remind the reader of my working definition of eco-spirituality: *Spirit connecting with spirit*. This divine life-force does not inhabit some idyllic habitat above and beyond this vale of tears; it dwells right here in the cosmic and planetary encounters of each day and moment. And, as the British theologian John Taylor wrote many years ago, such an encounter is not merely affirming and reassuring but can often be bewildering and even overwhelming:

> To think deeply about the Holy Spirit is a bewildering, tearing exercise, for whatever he touches, he turns it inside out. He gives himself in our most interior and private experiences and then shows that what we thought was our monopoly belongs to everybody. . . . For the Spirit, what is here is everywhere, yet would be nowhere were it not here. (Taylor 1972, 179)

"Our monopoly belongs to everybody." What might this phrase mean? I propose that this is the monopoly of God's *unconditional love* for all creation, from the macroscopic cosmic level right down to the minuscule subatomic particles. At the human level it is that bold, almost outrageous realization that *we are loved unconditionally*. In the New Testament we encounter this outreach of unconditional love in two main passages from the Johannine corpus:

> "A new commandment I give unto you, that you love one another; as I have loved you, may you also love one another." (Jn 13:34)

> "Beloved, let us love one another: for love is of God; and everyone who knows love is born of God, and knows God. The one that loves not, does not know God; for God is love. In this the love of God was made manifest among us, that God sent his only Son into the world, so that we might have life through him.

> Herein is love, not that we loved God, but that God
> loved us, and sent his Son to be the atoning sacrifice
> for our sins. Beloved, if God so loved us, we also
> should love one another. (1 Jn 4:7–11)

The originality and profundity of these statements has
long eluded Christians, because—like other major world
religions—religious belief is postulated upon meeting conditions and fulfilling the requirements of such conditions.
Over and over again the message, both subtle and overt,
has been that only by fulfilling your obligations to God
(and to the church) will you be acceptable to God and,
thus, capable of meriting God's love. Such love can only
be earned, and always at a price!

But the foundational "monopoly" is quite different, and this
is where spirituality and religion begin to part company. All
persons, irrespective of their religion—and indeed, all God's
creatures—are beneficiaries of this unconditional love. First,
therefore, we must strive to outgrow the false indoctrination
we have internalized over many centuries, gracefully and
gratefully begin to acknowledge the endowment of being
loved unconditionally, and, then, (hopefully) we can begin
to embrace the greatest "condition" of all: *just as we have
been unconditionally loved, we, too, must love unconditionally all other living creatures, human and nonhuman alike.*

There are two faces to this spirit-infused reality, what we
might broadly call the positive and negative, understood
as complementary rather than opposite characteristics.
Positively, we are beneficiaries of a universal giftedness;
this, more than anything else, is the conduit through which
we experience the endowment and enrichment of God's
unconditional love. Creation is one lavish gift, forever

liberating and empowering possibilities for becoming, which in secular language we describe as the process of evolution. Of course, we know only too well the negative; that evolution is not some kind of straight line, forever building on past successes while discarding those variants that are no longer useful (the survival of the fittest). It is a great deal more complex (see Johnson 2014), and it involves turbulence, chaos, destruction, decay, and death. Evolution is loaded with negative fallout, which, in a later chapter, I will describe as the great paradox.

These two features—positive and negative—are complementary forces within the trajectory of God's unconditional love. We cannot have one without the other. This paradoxical mix of light and darkness tends to be split and divided in several of the great religions, but in spirituality—and specifically in eco-spirituality—we hold both together, because the Great Spirit is creatively operating in and through both dimensions.

All Is Gift!

Organically and experientially we are born into a world of promise and potential, often scarred because of poverty, violence, and human greed. Despite the dark and oppressive shadow into which millions are born, let's begin by asserting what the creative God of unconditional love desires for all beings. Such an endowment of promise and hope is elegantly articulated by the biologist, Andreas Weber:

> In the natural world, everything is gifted. From the sun's warmth to the sustenance that it denotes to us, from the possibilities of deep self-understanding to the

joy that results from it, nature's gifts are exuded as
unconditional offerings. We receive everything living
free of charge. The vivacity that we experience in the
old, densely interwoven network of relationship is an
offering without expectation of return: an expression
of life that enlivens. . . . In the natural world, the most
complicated, most valuable things are given away
without a thought. Its abundance is not conducive
to investment but is an act of trust that is constantly
redeemed in a grandeur that seems senseless to frugal
capitalists like us. (Weber 2014, 182, 187)

When we review our human story in the context of deep
time, reclaiming the sphere of the hunter-gatherer and well
beyond it, it becomes all too clear that gift-giving has long
been one of the major forms of social exchange, encom-
passing multiple domains of social life and carrying rich
meanings above and beyond mere economic need. Moreover, anthropological studies of gift-giving reveal the social
origins of economic institutions and provide insights about
the value of human labor that have long been obscured by
modern economic theories.

I am not proposing a return to some idyllic past that,
truthfully, never existed. In keeping with the wisdom of
contemporary theology and scripture study, I am seeking to
rework the tradition by expanding it beyond Christianity's
classic bounds and into deep time, seeking to honor the full
scope of what the creative Spirit has been doing across the
billions of years of cosmic and planetary evolution, including the entire spectrum of human becoming. Our species
did not depart from the paradise of a long-lost garden.
We have emerged in connection with Spirit and our fellow
creatures over seven million years.

My endeavor is poetically captured in this chapter's opening quotation from British animist and philosopher Emma Restall Orr: "Our soul riding the current of the spirits whose perpetual motion is our becoming" (Orr 2012). Despite the many things going wrong in our world, amid so much unjust oppression, pain, and suffering, human beings still search and hunger for a wholeness we intuitively know to be real. It is the "oneness" desired by many of the great mystics, the non-dualism of Advaita Vedanta, the scientific pursuit of a theory of everything or a grand unified theory,[4] and the yearning of several pacifist and non-violent movements, including the establishment of the United Nations, for unifying governance for the planet.

These are just some of the indicators of the waves upon which the spirits are riding—the divine Spirit and our human spirits—in a perpetual evolutionary motion, seeking to co-create a new and different world for the benefit of all. In spite of all the negative forces to the contrary, this new world order continues to engage our species and will not let us go, no matter how much we try to resist it. In that hopeful defiance for a new world, we revisit the notion of eco-spirituality, with its dynamic, expansive horizon, to deliver a different kind of world more radiant with meaning and hope.

---

[4] A theory of everything would unify all the fundamental interactions of nature: gravitation, the strong interaction, the weak interaction, and electromagnetism. Several Grand Unified Theories (GUTs) have been proposed to unify electromagnetism and the weak and strong forces. A theory of everything (TOE), or a master theory, is a hypothetical, single, all-encompassing, coherent theoretical framework of physics attempting to explain fully and link together all physical aspects of the universe.

Critical Issues for Ongoing Discernment

1. Eco-spirituality transcends all formal religion and pre-dates formal religions by several thousands of years.
2. In eco-spirituality we seek to transcend and outgrow the dualistic splits between sacred and secular and between spirit and matter.
3. Eco-spirituality seeks to incorporate and integrate humanity's evolutionary story of seven million years, thus transcending the anthropology—understanding of the human—largely inherited from classical Greek philosophy and adopted by the major world religions.
4. The enlarged worldview from modern Western sciences—particularly cosmology, quantum science, and evolutionary unfolding—requires us to revisit the sense of oneness named by mystics down through the ages, enriching the potential of eco-spirituality as a world-transforming resource.
5. To engage the Spirit of God in a discerning way today, we need to embrace a multidisciplinary wisdom and not merely the monopoly of truth long held by formal religion.
6. Even our understanding of God will need to change—away from the ruling, patriarchal Father to the energizing Spirit who empowers everything from within.

2

Something Like a Paradigm Shift

Scientific thought shifted during the past decades from cosmology, the study of the way nature works, to Cosmo-genesis, the study of the way every existing thing in the universe originates from the Big Bang. . . . Obviously, ecological spirituality has deep roots in this renewed understanding of ongoing creation.

—Joseph A. Tetlow, SJ

Evolution, rooted in habits that provide stability, proceeds in quantum leaps.

—Judy Cannato

Almost thirty years ago, the United States Conference of Catholic Bishops issued a statement on ecological spirituality. The statement lists the following destructive behaviors of our human species: depletion of ozone, deforestation, contamination from toxic and nuclear wastes, global warming. It then issues this ethical challenge: "We are of the earth. We must treat it as we do our home. There is no true spirituality without obedience to this moral mandate" (Tetlow 1995).

"We are of the earth." That one simple phrase may well be one of the most revolutionary statements ever made by any religious leadership group anywhere in our world. The statement offers a further elaboration:

> Spirituality goes beyond moral action and transmutes it. Ecological spirituality begins in the acknowledgment, grateful and joyful, that all creatures owe their existence to God. Humans are not somehow separate from the rest of creation. We share it intimately with other creatures. We acknowledge God as Creator of us all. (Tetlow 1995)

Elsewhere we encounter yet another provocative statement: "Humans are not somehow separate from the rest of creation" (Tetlow 1995). One wonders if the US bishops themselves consistently preached and advocated this stance in the months and years after publishing the statement. Did they acknowledge and confront the inherited teaching, so long unquestioned, that Christians do not belong to this vale of tears, that we are creatures fundamentally alienated from God (by virtue of original sin), that, like the people of Israel, we are creatures in exile,[1] forever seeking to come home, and therefore we are called to separate from the natural world so that we can escape to true life in a world

---

[1] On the notion of exile in the Hebrew scriptures, theologian Francesca Stavrakopoulou claims that "although these texts tend to present the exile and return as the experience of all Judahites, this was not the case. Only the elites and some among the professional classes had been deported to Babylonia, and the majority remained there" (Stavrakopoulou 2021, 14). The notion of exile has been extensively—erroneously—used throughout the centuries to highlight the need to separate and distance ourselves from our earthiness.

beyond this sin-infested realm? Did the bishops even realize that they were advocating something akin to a paradigm shift in the very meaning of what constitutes human nature?

Although the Catholic Church is convinced of the endless interdependence between humanity and nature, it has always rejected biocentrism. According to Pope John Paul II,

> placing human well-being at the center of concern for the environment is actually the surest way of safeguarding creation; this in fact stimulates the responsibility of the individual with regard to natural resources and their judicious use. (John Paul II 1999)

Ten years later Pope Benedict XVI stated that technology

> *is a response to God's command to till and keep the land.* . . . I would advocate the adoption of a model of development based on the centrality of the human person, on the promotion and sharing of the common good, on responsibility, on a realization of our need for a changed lifestyle, and on prudence, the virtue which tells us what needs to be done today in view of what might happen tomorrow. (Benedict XVI 2010)

This is far removed, indeed, from deep ecology, which has always been critical of the Catholic Church's anthropocentric views.

However, in his acclaimed 2015 encyclical, *Laudato Si'*, Pope Francis moves beyond his predecessors, making the same assertion as that of the American bishops twenty years earlier: "Nature cannot be regarded as something separate from ourselves or as a mere setting in which we live. We are part of nature, included in it and thus in constant interaction with it" (Francis 2015, no. 139). One wonders to what extent the Catholic faithful—indeed, religious believers in general—have actually heard this message, internalized it, and started to live out of it with the substantial lifestyle changes that are involved.

Ecological spirituality has become a kind of clarion call for all religiously responsive humans of the twenty-first century. Such is the now precarious state of our earth, and the several environmental threats that are facing us, that every sphere of wisdom—including religion—feels compelled to act. As this urgent ecological and environmental agenda is calling forth a range of "trans-institutional" agencies and creative networks in the social, political, and economic spheres, so too in the religious domain. Beyond churches and mainline religions, we witness the rise of a wider amorphous movement in which people tend to identify as spiritual rather than religious. Among this wider network-ing sphere, we hear the strongest appeal for an ecological spirituality in our time.

From Escape to Engage

In the present work I plan to outline the central tenets and beliefs of this emerging movement. My primary concern, however, is to highlight what may best be described as a paradigm shift,[2] indicating the collapse of an older approach

---

[2] Richard Rohr (2019, 35–37) references the contemporary use of the term *paradigm shift* employed by the philosopher Thomas Kuhn and indicates its relevance for the shift in meaning taking place today in both spirituality and theology. As applied to contemporary theol-ogy, see Dirk-Martin Grube, "Christian Theology Emerged by Way of a Kuhnian Paradigm Shift," *International Journal of Philosophy and Theology* 79 (2018), 178–93. As applied to morality and ethics

in favor of something that seems radically new. This description holds several resonances with the contemporary evolutionary breakthroughs popularized by contemporary writers such as Ilia Delio, John F. Haught, and Carter Phipps. In 1998, Sr. Joan Chittister highlighted one central feature of this movement:

> There is a new question in the Spiritual Life; it is the spirituality of the Spiritual Life itself. Life here and the way we relate to it, rather than life to come and how we can guarantee it for ourselves, has become the spiritual conundrum of our age. (Chittister 1998, 1)

The quotation addresses two features of central importance: anthropology and worldviews. Personal identity is focused on the spiritual dimension of the soul, without which a human being is not a full person; and, at the end of the human lifespan on this earth, only the soul can be redeemed and saved. A robust spiritual life is deemed important, if not essential, to obtain such salvation.

The second feature—worldviews—correlates with the stated anthropology. It is only in the world hereafter, well away from this earthly vale of tears, that salvation can be achieved. And that is only possible after dying to our earthly reality. Here, we are dealing with a three-tier universe—heaven above, Hades or hell beneath, and the earth in between. Only the world above is deemed to be fully real, and it alone endures eternally. It is God's abode and full of the glory and power of God.

---

today, see Chet W. Sisk, "How the Current Paradigm Shift Is Changing Our Understanding of Ethics," *Tattva Journal of Philosophy* 6, no. 2 (2014): 45–59.

Although God created the entire world, only Planet Earth has any real value for humans, since it is into this sphere that Jesus comes to make salvation hereafter possible for humans. Admittedly, salvation can be achieved in and through our earthly situation, but only through the power of God, which itself transcends everything to do with the earthly creation.

Reflecting on this worldview, it sounds as though the earth were created as some kind of a testing ground for humans. It seems to be the only sphere in which humans can work out their salvation, yet it is full of potential hazards capable of distracting humans from their life's mission. Indeed, it is hard to avoid the conclusion that the almighty God is highly ambivalent regarding the earthly creation—and even more ambivalent regarding humans as earthly beings.

Or is it God who is ambivalent? Might it not be—as scripture scholar Wes Howard-Brook intimates—that humans themselves have created the ambivalence, pursuing a drive for power that they had assumed came from God, but that we can now see as coming from their own confused relationship with the organicity of the natural world? Wes Howard-Brook invites us to return to the opening chapter of Genesis and its resounding mantra: "And God saw that it was good." For Howard-Brook, that is the original "covenant," the foundational basis of all creativity, divine and human alike.

Unfortunately, as we move through the opening chapters of Genesis, we encounter a looming dark cloud of violence and patriarchal domination. Karen Armstrong succinctly captures the destructive mood when she writes:

The God who dominates the first chapter of the Bible has disappeared from the human scene by the end of Genesis. Story after story reveals a much more disturbing God: as we shall see the omnipotent God of the first chapter soon loses control of his creation; the immutable deity is seen to change his mind and even to feel threatened by humanity. The benevolent Creator becomes a fearful Destroyer. The impartial God who saw all his creatures as "good" now has favorites and teaches his protégés to behave in an equally unfair manner to their dependents. By the time we have reached the end of the text, almost every one of the expectations we were encouraged to form in Chapter 1 have been knocked down. (Armstrong 1996, 13)

For much of the rest of the Hebrew scriptures this violent imperial deity plays a leading role,[3] but we must note it is always at the behest of violent, power-hungry humans who are ever more convinced that they truly represent a power-mongering God. As several scholars have suggested, Jesus departs radically from this violent God-image in favor of the nonviolent strategy of the new reign of God (e.g., Crossan 2022; Sprinkle 2021; Wink 2003).

The clarion call to embrace the nonviolent creative God of Genesis 1 is quickly suffocated by what Howard-Brook describes as violent imperial divinity, or what postcolonial scholars of our time describe as colonial mimicry (O'Murchu

---

[3] In the oft-cited example from Jesuit scholar Raymund Schwager, "The Hebrew Bible contains 1,000 verses where God's own violent actions of punishment are described, 100 passages where Yahweh expressly commands others to kill people, and several stories where God kills or tries to kill for no apparent reason. Violence is easily the most often mentioned activity and central theme of the Hebrew Bible" (Schwager 1987, 60).

2014). As I shall indicate later, this portrayal of God and God's dealings with humanity is actually based on a range of human projections focused on the ideology of conquer and control, many elements of which were born out of the shadow side of the Agricultural Revolution and can be traced to around 10,000 BCE.

Civilization as Imperial Control

The enlarged cultural and earthly horizon of eco-spirituality incorporates scholarly research across Western academic areas, yet it has scarcely been incorporated by many of the religious traditions that we know today. Two strands of what we take to be "normal" are no longer sustainable and need to be revisited and reframed if we stand any hope of discerning the deeper meaning of ecological spirituality in our time. The first is our prevailing notion of civilization, and the second is that of divinely sanctioned imperialism.

As we revisit our notions of civilization, we must consider at least two outstanding features: containment and the ability to record. With the initial wave of agricultural development reaching its high point, our species largely abandoned its hunter-gatherer status and settled down into a more structured way of life. The Sumerian culture initially emerged around 5,000 BCE, located in the valleys of the Tigris and Euphrates rivers of southern Mesopotamia (present-day Iraq). Sumerian farmers grew an abundance of grain and other crops, the surplus from which enabled them to form urban settlements. By 3,000 BCE, writing was developed within the same context, reinforcing the desire to manage human affairs in an orderly, controlled manner.

On the surface that seems a responsible and rational way to manage human affairs, and it did reap enormous benefits for human progress and the evolution of our species. It also bore a subtle underlying aspiration, uprooting humans from a deep interconnection with the natural world that had sustained and inspired humans previously over several thousand years. In this new civilized domain humans were no longer earthlings in an integrated sense but progressively becoming superior beings for which earth and its resources were mere commodities to be used and managed in an ever-deepening rational mode. And with the emergence of such rationality, the human capacity for creativity, imagination, intuition, and spirituality became ever more compromised.[4]

Second, we must revisit divinely sanctioned imperialism. Paralleling the emergence of civilization as outlined above, divinely sanctioned imperialism strongly reinforces the growing tendency toward domination and control in human societies. For much of Christian history God has been understood as a ruling male king who created and ruled the world from a throne in a heavenly realm beyond the material creation. Some have argued for a scriptural basis for this claim, tracing monarchical theology to the great divinized kings of the Hebrew scriptures and recognizing the eminence of King David, the root from whom emerged Jesus Christ in his royal office.[5]

[4] Anthropologist David Graeber and archaeologist David Wengrow provide a fine overview of the cultural implications of these Sumerian-based developments (Graeber and Wengrow 2021).

[5] Presbyterian scholar Michael LeFebvre argues that, in God's plan, Adam should be understood not as the first human but as the first vice-regent (royal figurehead) representing God as King. See

Most scholarly investigation of the origins and meaning of divine kingship is based on Christian traditions, with possible influences through Judaism and from surrounding regions like Persia, Mesopotamia, and, especially, Egypt.[6] While divine kingship also occurred in other ancient cultures, including China, Japan, India, and in various African traditions, these receive scant attention in scholarly literature. Research based on Christian tradition seems to have exerted substantial influence far beyond its original historical and cultural context.

In his classic work *The Golden Bough*, James G. Frazer suggests that certain individuals of presumed magical/sacred powers enabled them to interact with the forces of nature and positively influence it, thus enabling them to earn the status of chiefs and kings in the first human societies (Frazer 1894). One of the consequences of their privileged contact with the forces of nature would have been concern for their physical condition, the fear that their degeneration would drag down the whole universe with it. To prevent this catastrophic hypothesis from becoming reality, it was thought necessary to anticipate the natural death of the king and kill him first. This would allow his soul to be transferred to a stronger successor, and his physical well-being would thus be harmoniously linked by means of the sympathetic principle of magic to that of the whole universe.[7]

Michael LeFebvre, "Adam Reigns in Eden: Genesis and the Origins of Kingship," *Bulletin of Ecclesial Theology* 5, no. 2 (2018): 25–57.

[6] As outlined in *Religion and Power: Divine Kingship in the Ancient World and Beyond* (Brisch 2008). This is a volume of scholarly papers presented during the Third Annual University of Chicago Oriental Institute Seminar held February 23–24, 2007.

[7] Frazer compiled *The Golden Bough* based on a great amount of data he collected over the years from various sources, including

Beyond the spiritual/religious significance of the ruling king, the relationship between sacred kingship and priestly cultic function occurs in several ancient cultures.[8] Furthermore, it features strongly in certain Christian traditions and prevails this day in the role of bishops, specifically in the Catholic understanding of the papacy.

Returning to Context

According to popular legend, King Sargon of Akkad was the world's first imperial ruler, establishing the Akkadian empire in Mesopotamia between 2334 and 2154 BCE. Despite several suggestions of the type outlined in Frazer's *The Golden Bough*, there is actually no substantial evidence to trace kingship—secular or religious—beyond 3000 BCE. The lack of evidence creates serious problems around both the meaning and veracity of formal religions as we know them

---

already written works on the topic of different cultures and reports from missionaries and travelers who were in direct contact with those cultures. He did not, however, travel extensively himself. When completed, *The Golden Bough* was an impressive compilation of customs, rituals, and beliefs of cultures around the world. Frazer particularly emphasized similarities of key themes, such as birth, growth, death, and rebirth, that he found across cultures. Through this, Frazer provoked new insights into cultural diversity and commonality, a different perspective in what had, until then, been European-centered and American-centered academia. His work inspired the understanding of divine kingship, the combination of monarchy and priesthood, and the concept of the sacrificial killing of the "Year King" by his successor, in a rite of renewal.

[8] The strict separation of the priestly office from that of the king, as in India, where king and priest belong to different castes—Kshatriya and Brahman, respectively—is an unusual exception.

today, since the validation of divine kingship is extensively invoked as the foundation of such religions.

The focus on a patriarchal ruling God within the culture of formal religion seems to have evolved within a historical period when human consciousness was strongly focused on what we today call imperial power. In the wake of the Agricultural Revolution, the stratification and management of land was well established, as was the primacy of male domination, leading to the cultural development of patriarchal management and male dominance. Additionally, the emerging mindset, particularly among those pursuing hierarchical, imperial power, was that of the use of "reason" as philosophical rationality, reaching its fuller articulation in the works of Plato and Aristotle. Inevitably, religion became ensconced in this imperial paradigm and supported its desire to conquer and control for the ruling God.

All of which brings us to a central question for the present work: How was the human relationship with God understood and expressed before monarchical imperialism? With the stratification of the land in the Agricultural Revolution, the egalitarian nature of the hunter-gatherer lifestyle waned considerably.[9] Moreover, we are relying largely on mythology to access what the spirituality of these hunter-gatherers was like. Several contemporary Indigenous groups adopt a lifestyle generally assumed to be similar to the hunter-gatherers of earlier times; at best we can only

---

[9] In terms of the alleged egalitarianism of hunter-gatherers, I tend to follow the British anthropologist James Woodburn (1970), considered by Graeber and Wengrow (2021, 128ff.), among others, to be the greatest modern authority on this ancient creative collaboration.

draw tentative conclusions as all contemporary peoples are affected by the consciousness of our time, irrespective of their externalized behaviors.

We have some valuable studies on shamanism and its spiritual significance going back some twenty thousand years. The shaman or shamaness is often portrayed as being similar to the priest, a mediator between God and the people. That comparison sounds like a projection from our time onto a phenomenon of a previous era, long predating the evolution of priesthood as we know it today. The evidence suggests that the shaman was called forth by the community to act as a healer and ritual animator on behalf of the community. The shaman or shamaness represents a holiness arising from within the community itself rather than one related to a distant deity or to the imperial system out of which priesthood initially evolved.

For much of this book I draw inspiration for a paradigm of spirituality not merely as a pre-religious phenomenon, nor as one based uniquely on the hunter-gatherer culture (although it may well have been prevalent in that context), but as a way of engaging the world that becomes ever more transparent in our evolving creativity as a human species. This takes us into the realm of "deep time," a context frequently ridiculed and dismissed by contemporary scholarship (secular and religious) as nostalgic, utopian, speculative, and completely unacceptable in terms of the rigorous scientific objectivity of our "civilized" world!

The creativity I am referencing is becoming an ever-more-rigorous pursuit among anthropologists, archaeologists, and social historians. It is very much an emergence of the latter half of the twentieth century and still remains largely unknown to the academic world generally and to the cultural environment of the major world religions. I will outline the details in subsequent chapters.

Embracing an Enlarged Horizon

Among the religions—and our churches—one often encounters a resistance to any talk about spirituality in this mode or indeed to the more general notion of creativity. Such conversation feels like a threat to those who feel they have a monopoly over such spiritual truth, that its authentic nature is only accessible in and through a tradition that has stood the test of time. But what time scales are envisaged here? As outlined above, they belong largely if not exclusively to the restricted context of the past five thousand years.

There is also a Darwinian dynamic at work here. When Darwinian theory advocates the survival of the fittest (a phrase coined by Herbert Spencer), it suggests that organisms best adjusted to their environment are the most successful in surviving and reproducing. In this understanding, nature is driven by selfish genes forever seeking their own advancement. There is, however, a further nuance to this theory: those variants from the past that have stood the test of time can be best trusted to carry life forward into richer and more useful forms. Success based on the past is the best guarantee for a better future. The past is more reliable than the future.

Formal religions, consciously or otherwise, fully support this conviction. God's revelation for us is in truths embedded in historical scriptures and practices that have endured over time. According to religionists of a more fundamentalist persuasion, foundational doctrines such as those of the Trinity, the divinity of Jesus, and the nature of the church can never be abandoned or even altered. They are essentially immutable, like God! In such contexts authentic spirituality is that which clings as closely as possible to the inherited truths, often to the point of interpreting the scriptures literally. The legacy being referenced here is that of the past five thousand years or, in several cases, the past two thousand years.

The evolutionary momentum of the twenty-first century is progressively undermining this allegiance to a fixed, enduring past of a mere few thousand years. John Haught is among the scholars who have challenged this view most directly. Developing the notion from Pierre Teilhard de Chardin that evolution leads us forth into ever deeper levels of complexity, Haught claims that such momentum is not merely driven from the past but also responds to what he describes as "the lure of the future" (Haught 2010; 2015).

For Haught, the pull toward the future is at least as important as reliance on the past—in fact, probably more significant. Haught argues his case on a theological basis, recognizing the God who forever promises new life (fullness of life) and always fulfills the promises. This is very much a faith perspective, verging on a kind of mystical trust that defies any sense of rational reason.[10] His argument becomes much more coherent theologically and spiritually if we postulate the Spirit who blows where it wills (see Jn 3:8) as the one who lures forward the whole creation into that fullness of life that every religion claims to be its ultimate goal.

---

[10] This mystical trust is sometimes described as eco-mysticism, as explored by American medical-spiritual explorer Carl Von Essen (2010).

Now, my earlier description of spirituality as Spirit connecting with spirit takes on even a more profound meaning, and the evolutionary implications, as outlined by another contemporary scholar, Sr. Ilia Delio, become a great deal clearer. We are now entering an enlarged horizon of our understanding of God and of how that same God, as energizing and creative Spirit, invites us into a deeper and wider engagement with the whole creation. We are dealing with what several Indigenous Peoples around our world call the Great Spirit.

Embracing the Paradigm Shift

To some, the emerging paradigm I describe above will feel like abandoning all that we have long considered to be sacrosanct and beyond challenge. In these established paradigms, as ensouled beings, we were never meant to be at home on the earth. The whole point of a spiritual life was to maintain a steady growth into transcendence, leaving behind all earthly attachments, so that the soul becomes ever more unencumbered to escape the entrapment of the earthly body and unite with God in the heavenly realm—the only true home of all human destiny.

In some Jewish and Christian contexts the very notion of humans being ensouled is largely the ingenious idea of the Greek philosophers Plato and Aristotle. The inheritance of their insights are a mere twenty-five-hundred years old. What constituted human ensoulment before that time, over the long evolutionary story of some seven million years, as upheld by the contemporary study of human origins? Several multidisciplinary studies now highlight that it was our deep immersion in the earth—as earthlings—that begot, nurtured, and sustained our meaning as spiritual beings. The notion of being inhabited by a divinely endowed soul arises from a dualistic split largely unknown to our ancient ancestors. This splitting between the sacred and secular has humans today in the spiritual crisis we are enduring.

And it is a great deal more than a spiritual emergency. It is a crisis of identity. What now constitutes the core of our being if the notion of ensoulment is no longer credible? What does it mean—humanly, socially, and spiritually—to identify anew as earthlings? Who or what is the God we encounter in the interior landscape of this divine-earthly encounter? Hopefully the reflections of this book will offer some answers to these foundational questions for the new horizons of discernment emerging in our time.

Critical Issues for Ongoing Discernment

1. "There is a new question in the spiritual life: It is the spirituality of the spiritual life itself. Life here and the way we relate to it, rather than life to come and how we can guarantee it for ourselves, has become the spiritual conundrum of the age." (Chittister 1998, 1)
2. For much of this book I draw inspiration for a paradigm of spirituality focused on a way of engaging the world—and not just church or religion—that becomes ever more transparent in our evolving creativity as a human species.
3. "Nature cannot be regarded as something separate from ourselves or as a mere setting in which we live. We are part of nature, included in it and thus in constant interaction with it." (Francis 2015, no. 139).
4. Both religion and spirituality prioritize the spiritual dimension of our selves (the soul) as superior to all other aspects, particularly our earthly identity. Eco-spirituality prioritizes our earthiness as the primary sphere in which God's Spirit operates, thus inviting us to reclaim the foundational sacredness of our identity as earthlings.
5. Throughout this book I define spirituality as *Spirit connecting with spirit.* I am adopting an understanding of God as an energizing and creative Spirit, inviting us into a deeper and wider engagement with the whole creation and not merely with church or religion.

3

In the Beginning Was the Spirit

Whenever I learn a little more of the processes of creation I am amazed afresh at the unbelievable daring of the Creator Spirit who seems to gamble all the past gains on a new initiative, inciting his creatures to such crazy adventure and risk.

—John V. Taylor

We know now from quantum physics that matter is simply fields of force made sense by the spirit of Energy.

—Joan Chittister

The first chapter of Genesis portrays a God who creates, according to Christian classical theism, *ex nihilo* (from nothing). This deity is the One before whom nothing existed, the originator and sustainer of everything in creation. We have long assumed that this creative act was the first of any type of creativity anywhere in creation, but the claim for the divine *ex nihilo* tells virtually nothing about creation itself and a great deal about the One who creates as it was understood at the time.

Creatio ex nihilo (creation from nothing) is a patriarchal theological assertion for a creating, sustaining, and ruling

God beyond whom nothing ever did exist or could exist. He is the absolute Lord of all creation, creating the world from the source of his infinite power. Nothing was possible before him, and nothing is possible beyond him. Such an exalted status is meant to draw forth the kind of adulation expressed in phrases such as "To him be honor, power, and glory for ever and ever. Amen."

Yet such divine attributions originate as metaphysical projections in classical Greek philosophy, too long assumed to provide reliable access to God's real nature, rather than the scriptural record. In *creatio ex nihilo,* the absolute unquestioned power of human patriarchy itself is at stake, not a revelation into the nature of God. Fortunately, the divine nature is well beyond the power of human rationality and the pursuit of domination that follows. When engaging the God-question from within the realm of spirituality, then, we must inhabit a humbler space, progressively beginning to realize that the space of creation itself provides a more authentic route to the meaning and mystery we call God.

The Energizing Spirit

A more discerning analysis of Genesis 1 opens us up to other creative possibilities that provide rich insights for eco-spirituality today. The NRSV Catholic Edition reads:

> In the beginning when God created the heavens and the earth, the earth was a formless void and darkness covered the face of the deep, while a wind from God swept over the face of the waters. (Gen 1:1–2)

But another translation of the original Hebrew is possible:

> At the beginning of God's creating of the heavens and
> the earth, when the earth was wild and waste [tohu
> va-vohu], darkness over the face of Ocean, breath of
> God hovering over the face of the waters, God said:
> Let there be light. (Everett Fox 1983, 11)

Twenty years after Everett Fox's translation, Catherine
Keller plumbs scholarly and discerning depths to indicate
that the divine force at work is not the creator Father but
the energizing Spirit, which Christians name the Holy Spirit
of God (Keller 2003). *Creatio ex nihilo* scarcely touches or
illumines the primordial depths into which the Spirit reaches.
"What if," asks Keller, "we begin instead from the vantage
point of fecund multiplicity, its flux into flesh, its overflow
. . . in a creation narrative as a textured process of energy
flows?" (Keller 2003, 19, 236). Here, she is alluding to the
Energy (with capitalized E) cited in this chapter's opening
quotation from Sr. Joan Chittister.

Without this primordial creative and empowering energy,
not even the Father God can create from the exclusive and
dominant realm of *creatio ex nihilo*. The breath of God
hovering over the face of the waters, drawing forth coher-
ence from the explosive chaos—the quantum vacuum of
contemporary physics—is the foundational source of all
evolutionary becoming (Keller 2003). Throughout the
universe, we know.

We undermine this foundational truth by our tendency
to interpret the opening of John's Gospel literally: "In
the beginning was the Word . . . and the Word was God"
(Jn 1:1). The Greek word used is *Logos*, which literally
means the rational principle through which everything can
be rationally explained. The Hellenistic (Greek) influence is

clearly discernible, and it is quite probable that the author of John's Gospel was evoking God "pronouncing" creation into being in the opening chapter of Genesis.

Yet, as highlighted by Steven R. Service and Catherine Keller, reading Greek philosophical notions of rationality back onto the Hebrew seriously undermines the creative dynamism inherent in the ancient Hebrew (Service 2015, 59ff.; Keller 2003, 60–64). The Greek epistemological principle of non-contradiction leaves us with a conceptual and linguistic overload that is unable to grasp the creative and dynamic empowerment that is communicated in the Hebrew scriptures. Though not appearing until later in Genesis, the Hebrew reference to the Divine Word, *dabar*, is used in an active sense, as a word event or prophetic word. The *dabar* of the Lord carries with it the ability to accomplish what it is sent to do, connoting a dynamism that is filled with a power that is felt by those who receive it yet remains present independent of such reception.

Service provides a detailed analysis of how *dabar* is used in the Hebrew scriptures, noting that "encounter with the *dabar* implied impartation of the Spirit" (Service 2015, 74n117). In different books of the Hebrew scriptures—for example, Psalms, Proverbs, and Jeremiah—the creation is expressly declared to be the work of Wisdom, for which *dabar* (the Word as action) is frequently used. And the holy *dabar* is uniquely manifested in the unfolding of creation: The heavens declare the glory of God as the world manifests or reveals the Holy One to our experience.

According to Service, the Hebrew *Dabar,* the Aramaic *Memra,* the Greek *Logos* (divine rational principle), and the Greek *Rhema* (utterance or things said) all communicate the Shekinah, the Presence of God, as a dynamic, empowering, creative life-force, identified primarily with that divine source we call the Holy Spirit of God (Service 2015, 46, 74, 99, 178–179, 458, 532). Furthermore, Service identifies the unfolding of this creative wisdom with the notion of the kingdom of God found in the Christian scriptures (Service 2015, 77, 197). The foundational empowering and dynamic relationality of the ancient Hebrew wisdom was subverted by the Greek desire for logic and rationality. Cold, hard fact took precedence over the mobile, amorphous flow of the Spirit's energy, begetting the empowering story of creation that science is making ever more transparent for our time.

Process theologian Ronald Faber, following the pioneering work of Alfred North Whitehead, suggests that we should understand the story of creation aesthetically rather than causally, with God as the poet of the world, erotically luring creation toward self-creativity (Faber 2004, 298). Supporting this view, Elizabeth Johnson writes:

A Creator Spirit dwells at the heart of the natural world, graciously energizing its evolution from within, compassionately holding all creatures in their finitude and death, and drawing the world forward toward an unimaginable future. Through the vast sweep of cosmic and biological evolution, the Spirit embraces the material root of life and its endless new potential, empowering the cosmic process from within. The universe, in turn is self-organizing and self-transcending, energized from the spiralling galaxies to the double helix of the DNA molecule, by the dance of divine vivifying power. (Johnson 2007, 191)[1]

---

[1] More recently, she has written: "God's Spirit breathes the world into being, dwells in all things, quickens love into flame, inspires the prophets, and renews the face of the earth" (Johnson 2018, 171).

Religious traditions beyond the Christian narrative also recognize this spiritual depth. According to Karen Armstrong, the ancient Vedic notion of *Rta* can be translated as "the artfulness of being" (Armstrong 2022, 46). In the ancient Chinese (Confucian) worldview, we encounter *Qi (Chi)*, often described as the vital essence of all things (Kim 2011). The *Dao* of Daoism may be more widely known and is understood as endlessly emanating from the divine unknown.[2]

Enter the Great Spirit

According to our inherited Christian narrative, the story of creation follows a descending hierarchical process from the Father, through the Son, and then the Holy Spirit, whose primary role is the creation of the church for the salvation of humankind. The Holy Spirit, as the third person of the Trinity, can only fulfill its role after the creating Father and the redeeming Son have done their work.

American theologian Mark I. Wallace suggests that it is time for a reversal of this convenient hierarchy (Wallace 2018). Rather than placing nature at our disposal, it is now the natural world itself, in all its power and poverty, its grandeur and fragility, that disposes us to interact with it as co-partners. For some years now Wallace has been describing this new sense of pneumatology as a biocentric redefinition of the Spirit as God's agent of interdependence and unity within all creation. The Spirit in our time is calling us to engage our own earthiness as the primary experiential

---

[2] All these concepts are employed and extensively explored by historian of world religions Karen Armstrong in her inspiring work on our need to rediscover the sacredness of nature faced with the major ecological challenges of our age (Armstrong 2022).

realm for the flourishing of that same spirit-infused creativity rather than merely becoming resource stewards of a creation that faces serious ecological challenges like the climate emergency. Our mission now is to become friends of the earth.

This earth-affiliated understanding of the Holy Spirit can be traced back to the mid-twentieth century through Christian scholars such as Wolfhart Pannenberg, Jürgen Moltmann, Elisabeth Schüssler-Fiorenza, Rosemary Radford Ruether, Denis Edwards, Elizabeth Johnson, Leonardo Boff, and others. In the present work I have noted parallels with the other great world religions. In the rest of this chapter I provide a brief overview of an even more ancient, deeper source: *the faith of Indigenous Peoples* around our world, whose understanding of God, or the power of the divine, can be encapsulated in the notion of the Great Spirit.[3] Once more, let me remind the reader of my basic definition of spirituality: *Spirit connecting with spirit*!

For the world's Indigenous Peoples, the Great Spirit is not so much a transcendent, personal being, as conventionally understood through Christian narratives, but a transpersonal energy force imbuing all creation with empowering creativity. Access to the Great Spirit is obtained through the land—not to be confused with either pantheism or panentheism. As earthlings, born out of the living earth and forever dependent on it for survival and flourishing, we come to know the Great Spirit through our convivial relationship with creation at large. In this context Indigenous Peoples do not necessarily worship the Great Spirit; rather, they forever strive to work collaboratively with the Spirit. Such

---

[3] I explored this topic at length in a previous work (see O'Murchu 2011).

collaboration is mediated mainly through rites and rituals, many of which are focused on the fertility of soil and land.

Our Western conditioning around the notion of a personal God—based on a largely unexamined anthropology—significantly impedes our ability to discern the deeper meaning of this Indigenous faith system. As conceptualized by Indigenous Peoples around the world, the notion of the Great Spirit is not personal in our normal adoption of that identity as used in religious language. Because of past dualistic indoctrination, we all too quickly conclude that we are dealing with a cold *impersonal* encounter, largely devoid of personalist significance. But this is not how Indigenous Peoples experience the Great Spirit. They neither think nor feel in terms of dualistic, binary distinctions. The Spirit that inhabits and energizes everything in creation is a life-force that embraces all that is deeply human while simultaneously transcending all our human categorizations.

To appreciate and comprehend this Indigenous wisdom, we need to acknowledge and confront possible underlying prejudices, not merely the racist/classicist dismissal of these people as being backward or uncivilized, but rather our inability to enter their perceptual world. They tend to judge and evaluate not through rational discourse but by "feeling for" and "feeling through" their experience. Our rational world is quick to dismiss such engagement as solipsistic, sentimental, narcissistic, and emotional. However, it is another way of understanding *Spirit connecting with spirit*, the depths of which are largely unexplored in the world's formal religions as popularly understood today.

Once again, science comes to our rescue, particularly the new biology as highlighted by German biologist Andreas Weber, who writes:

> Stated simply, the new biology considers the phenom-
> enon of feeling as the primary explanation not only
> of consciousness, but of all life processes. By "feeling"
> I mean the inner experience of meaning. . . . Feeling
> is much more basic and existential. It is an experi-
> ence and a formative power that binds an organism
> together. . . . Feeling without matter is impossible.
> What we experience inwardly as emotion is something
> that happens outwardly to ourselves as bodies. (Weber
> 2016, 4, 96)[4]

Experientially, belief in the notion of the Great Spirit is not centered in dogmas, conceptual beliefs, canonical approval, or fixed liturgies. Neither is it reserved to sacred buildings or divinely sanctioned hierarchies. It is a feeling engagement with the living, organic earth itself. By this deeper, feeling-based engagement with the living earth, humans grow more deeply into their God-endowed status as earthlings.

When we engage the notion of the Great Spirit as the entry point for accessing the divine imperative, several of our inherited religious beliefs are no longer sustainable. If we put the Spirit, the original energetic source of creativity evidenced in the opening verses of Genesis, first, then we need to reframe and reconfigure our understanding of God as Trinity. The Father/Creator can only create in the power of the energizing Spirit. As I indicate in another work

---

[4] Elsewhere Weber further elaborates: "Feelings are the barometer of aliveness within us" (Weber 2014, 145ff.). Related to these reflections is the work of Glenn Albrecht, retired Australian professor of sustainability, who explores new categories of human feelings arising from a more emotional grounding in nature's own feelings (Albrecht 2019).

(O'Murchu 2017), such a creative force is better understood through the metaphor of the *Great Birther* rather than the Great Ruler. In this reframing we can rescue Jesus from the anthropocentric Son of the ruling Father and revise his role within the African notion of the *Ancestors*, Jesus being an archetypal figure who reconnects humans with our great ancestral African story, going back some seven million years (O'Murchu 2008).

For many readers the most disturbing feature of this move is my claim that the Great Spirit is the primary energizing force at work in creation. In this approach the Great Spirit, not Jesus, becomes the foundational, archetypal articulation of God at work in creation. The Spirit's embodiment of the divine is not some transcendent, ethereal phenomenon above and beyond the material creation. To the contrary, the living earth itself is a vibrating, dynamic organism, energized by the creative energy of the Great Spirit. In other words, the revealed truth and presence of the divine reaches us through the living earth itself. Our earthiness is the umbilical cord linking us to the source of our holiness (read: wholeness), through the earth, not in spite of it, and certainly not beyond it. In brief, our earthiness is the royal road to deep incarnation.[5]

Spirituality, on the other hand, begins with the Great Spirit, that cosmic insinuation that energizes and empowers every movement within and around us. At one time deeply personal, but also transpersonal (as distinct from impersonal),

---

[5] The christological implications will be reviewed in Chapter 9 herein. Meanwhile, I reference the frequent allusions adopted by the late Marcus Borg describing Jesus as a Spirit-filled person (Marcus Borg, *Jesus, the Life, Teachings and Relevance of a Religious Revolutionary* (New York: Harper One, 2015).

the Great Spirit is both narrator and narrative of creation's evolving story. That outflow of the Spirit's creative potentiality requires a new vocabulary to capture some sense of its empowering possibilities. *Consciousness,* therefore, could be understood as the Spirit's wisdom that animates and sustains the underlying, enduring creativity. Here, foundational concepts overlap: Spirit, spirituality, energy, consciousness, and wisdom. Metaphysical distinction is irrelevant here. In a quantum universe, where everything is entangled, connectedness, not the clarity of separation, really matters.

Process theologian Roland Faber expresses something of that deeply entwined mystical nature of that foundational creativity well when he writes:

> It is in the ecological embedding and wholeness that the "spiritual" aspect of the spirit resides. This spirit acquires concreteness, however, not through reason, consciousness, or the freedom of decision . . . but through its preconscious spontaneity and unconscious feeling, its inclination towards intensity and its ecstatic causality, its mutual interpenetration of mentality and corporeality, potentiality and actuality, subjectivity and objectivity, subjective inwardness and rigorous self-surpassing—and all of these things within a specific ecological intertwinement. (Faber 2004, 287)[6]

---

[6] Similar sentiments are expressed by theologian Leonardo Boff in this inspiring quotation: "Everything having to do with the force of fascination, attraction, and union, with the solidarity that includes all, with the forgiveness that reconciles, with the communion that bonds and reconnects all, with creative fantasy, innovation, invention, creation, extrapolation, transcendence, ecstasy, newness, complexity, order, beauty, and with the most varied forms of life, has to do with the Spirit" (Boff 2013, 34).

The Ecological Spirit

This chapter is an attempt to establish and clarify a foundational tenet of eco-spirituality, namely, the central role of God as Spirit. It does not begin with God the Father, or with Jesus, but with the Holy Spirit.[7] Spiritually and theologically we are dealing with dislocation and relocation. Beyond the established metaphysical categories within which Christian theology (and spirituality) has evolved over the past two thousand years, we are moving in a much more mobile, process-type environment. The invitation to transcend the dogmatic certainties of the past in favor of a more exploratory seeking and searching is emerging here, opening us up to ever-enlarging horizons of meaning and creative possibility.

A second major shift of focus, even more dislocating perhaps than the altered understanding of God, is the deep affiliation and integration with the earth itself. In and through our *earthiness* we engage and embrace the work of the Spirit. As *Laudato Si'* notes: "Nature cannot be regarded as something separate from ourselves or as a mere setting in which we live. We are part of nature, included in it and thus in constant interaction with it" (Francis 2015, no. 139). The natural world, in all its wonder and beauty, and in all its perplexity and paradox, is our primary space for the divine encounter and the primary wellspring for our graced empowerment.

---

[7] I acknowledge that there are several theological conundrums here which I briefly reviewed in a previous work (O'Murchu 2021). In terms of linking our care for the earth with Jesus and the Gospels, Canadian theologian Norman Wirzba offers a range of insightful connections particularly in his works *Food and Faith* (Wirzba 2019) and *Agrarian Spirit* (Wirzba 2022).

Within our planetary-cosmic context, another shift of paradigmatic significance emerges. Our inherited sense of *aliveness* needs to be reconsidered and redefined. Everything energized by the Spirit of God carries a quality of aliveness that defies human attempts at strict definition or limiting description. There is no hierarchical ordering in what constitutes such aliveness, for the same animating energy births and sustains the herb, the plant, the animal, the mountain, and the human person. Each is uniquely endowed, and none is superior.

This marks a substantial departure from our inherited anthropology, which views humans as endowed with a soul, conferring a divinely imbued sacredness above and beyond all other creatures, and requiring humans to be viewed as over against the material creation, which can be a serious distraction from living in a more soulful way. Related to such an outmoded anthropology, humans are ensouled beings who do not really belong to this earthly abode. Earth becomes a realm of "exile" where we live out our existence until the soul is delivered from the earthly material body in death and can escape to the heavenly (soul-filled) realm, enjoying eternal life forever.

For eco-spirituality, the notion of the soul inhabiting the body (inherited from Plato and Aristotle) circumvents and undermines the sacredness humans have known across the seven million years of evolutionary unfolding. During all that time Spirit was at work within and around us, animating and influencing our conscious awareness. We would have intuited a feeling of being spirit beings without any of the baggage of the dualistic split between soul and body, spirit and matter, categories we have only known for the past few thousand years.

The spirituality of escape no longer makes human or theological sense, despite the fact that millions still adhere to it and invest their hope in a liberation beyond this vale of tears. This desire to escape contributes to the eco-anxiety arising among us today. Evolution is inviting and luring us toward a deeper and empowering mode of engagement—not with the distant God in a far-away heavenly sphere, but with the Holy One who invites us into encounter in the here and now, amid all the messy and promising realities of our earthly abode. The realization that this is what Jesus wanted from the very beginning, not merely for Christians but for all humanity, may be even more difficult for practicing Christians to accept.

As we continue to deepen and clarify the implications of shifting from our inherited sense of spirituality to the emerging landscape of the eco-spiritual, these inspiring words from theologian Shelly Rambo hopefully will encourage us to stay the pace: "The Spirit is defined by its movement not by its essence. The Spirit is the vibration, the flow, the flight and the unfolding of God that is unending and unconfining" (Rambo 2010). Let us venture further into that expanding horizon.

Critical Issues for Ongoing Discernment

1. Spirituality, as distinct from religion, begins with the creativity of God's Spirit, calling into being the entire creation: "A Creator Spirit dwells at the heart of the natural world. Through the vast sweep of cosmic and biological evolution, the Spirit embraces the material root of life and its endless new potential, empowering the cosmic process from within" (Johnson 2007, 191).

2. The Spirit in our time is calling us not merely to become stewards of creation facing serious ecological challenges like the climate emergency, but to engage our own earthiness as the primary experiential realm for the flourishing of that same spirit-infused creativity.

3. The Spirit referenced here is what Christians call the Holy Spirit, whose deeper meaning can be reclaimed through the Indigenous notion of the Great Spirit, in which the Spirit of God connects with humans primarily through the earth, soil, and land, rather than through the transcendent presence postulated by mainline religions.

4. Belief in the notion of the Great Spirit is not centered in dogmas, conceptual beliefs, canonical approval, or fixed liturgies. Rather it is a feeling-based engagement with the sacredness of the living earth, within which humans are called to grow more deeply into their God-endowed status as earthlings.

5. Eco-spirituality moves beyond our inherited notions of spirituality, exploring a deeper more integrated

relationship with God as living Spirit at the heart of creation. The dualistic split between sacred and secular is no longer meaningful.

4

Spirituality and Human Origins

We are projects of collective self-creation. What if we approached human history that way? What if we treat people from the beginning as imaginative, intelligent, playful creatures who deserve to be understood as such!

—David Graeber and David Wengrow

Humans, both as individuals and as communities, are embedded in a world of dense symbolic landscapes, and much of that is religious.

—Agustin Fuentes

Myths of origin abound in ancient and modern folklore alike.[1] Many are heavily influenced by the major religions

---

[1] Throughout this book I use the notion of myth to denote a type of narrative that occurs transculturally in our human search for meaning, stories that cannot be dismissed as fictional tales or superstitious legends, but rather are highly symbolic narratives into which we are drawn intellectually and emotionally, consciously and unconsciously. When a myth is working, it creates an idealized picture that seeks a worldview that is relatively coherent, harmonious, sensible, and, therefore, meaningful, so that life seems worth living. Although somewhat dated, the short and comprehensive overview of renowned anthropologist Claus Levi-Strauss (d. 1992) is still valuable (see Levi-Strauss 1978). For the general reader, I recommend McIntosh (2004), and the insightful overview of Armstrong (2022).

we know today. Not surprisingly, therefore, they tend to begin with God creating the world and designating humans—particularly males—with responsibility for the ongoing development of the universe. In many cases the idyllic start quickly becomes problematic. Humans begin to falter and fail. They resort to violence and begin vying with one another for godlike supremacy. Frequently, God "himself" becomes insinuated in the violence, eventually requiring some form of a divine scapegoat to get humans back on track and save the world from ultimate destruction. This is a myth of falling from idyllic life, searching for restoration, and a divinely initiated restoration amid risks of tremendous devastation.

This three-movement story suggests an anthropology that is not in keeping with contemporary evolutionary scientific understandings of the human person or our species, *Homo sapiens*. The notion of an original utopian state in which all humans coexisted in harmonic innocence makes no sense in an evolutionary universe. It is a deluded belief based on the notion of an omnipotent, perfect God as postulated by monotheism and Greek metaphysics that, in turn, postulates an original perfect human alongside the all-powerful Deity. In the second movement, a hunger for power marks a primordial irruption of the human urge for absolute control. Creation at large becomes a mere commodity for human usufruct.

Steve Taylor describes this new emergence as *the ego explosion*, representing a post-agricultural consciousness, with humans behaving as a superior species, seeking to control everything within and around them (Taylor 2005). In evolutionary terms this consciousness belongs to the past ten thousand years and may not be much older than six thousand years. Humans try to obtain that power by setting up a demonized, dualistic force with which we can engage in battle. Such dualistic splitting belongs to classical Greek times and may be no more than twenty-five-hundred years old. The heavenly battle, therefore, is a mirror image of the earthly strategy of competitive conflict adopted by patriarchal males in order to reclaim their power. Pride and disobedience become the primary sins that preoccupy this patriarchal myth, suggesting that formal religion is another central feature in the mythic interpretation. Here, we encounter another cultural landmark that dates back to about thirty-five-hundred years ago. Finally, in terms of the growth and flourishing of the human, the dichotomy between power and powerlessness controls and pollutes the entire plot. Most people will end up trapped in powerlessness and therefore can never hope to realize the fuller potential of their God-given humanity.

Human Origins Reconsidered

Myths are useful to explore and understand how we once viewed the world and lived within it. When myths are taken literally, and particularly when they are aligned with religious dogma, they tend to become preposterous ideologies. They ingrain cultural narratives in restrictive timescales and cultural bottlenecks, stifling and stultifying organic evolutionary growth.

While some myths of human origin leave the possible dating quite open, none of them allows for the possibility of an evolving species that today belongs to a narrative of *seven million years*.[2] The Toumai skull, unearthed in Chad, North

---

[2] Paleontologists who study human origins distinguish between the hominin species categories of *Australopithecus* and *Homo*. The

Africa, in 2000 CE, is the primary evidence for this date.[3]
Though an ancestral genus of hominin, the Toumai skull
demonstrates that we have been on the earth, evolving and
even flourishing throughout that entire time. The underlying
science is persuasive and rigorously pursued. The cultural and
spiritual significance has a great deal of catching up to do.

In the 1960s, American anthropologist F. Clark Howell
proposed the creation of a field that would examine human
evolution from all perspectives, using the term *paleoanthropology* to describe the field research he was doing west of
the Omo River in southern Ethiopia. Howell, along with
Richard Leakey from Kenya and Camille Arambourg from
France, led an international team investigating human evolution in the Shungura Formation, a composite geological
sequence spanning the past four million years. This was
done through detailed geological mapping of sedimentary
rock exposures and subsequent field collection of fossils
and archeological remains.[4]

------

former may be described as the proto-human, endowed with all the
potentialities to become authentically human. The status associated
with *Homo* is considered very close to what we are today. It is defined
by three features: walking upright, creative use of stone tools, and
a brain size of approximately 1473 cm³. This evolutionary status
tends to be dated back to 3.3 million years ago. Throughout the
present work I cite the date of human origins as seven million years
ago on the understanding that we, then, had the potential to become
more truly human. According to several contemporary scholars, the
distinction between the two is merely a blur.

[3] The study of human origins largely belongs to the second half
of the twentieth century and continues apace up to our own time.
Several web pages provide further detail, many designed in engagingly creative ways.

[4] Ancient plant and animal remains, as well as sediments, provided
paleo-environmental data. Changes in types of mammals over time
were used for dating (biostratigraphy), as was the measurement of

The study of human evolution has a relatively recent history. The first fossil remains, those of the European Neanderthals, were only identified as such in the mid-nineteenth century (Papagianni and Morse 2013). The first ancient African hominids, the australopithecines, were discovered in the 1920s (Dart 1925); *Sahelanthropus tchadensis* is one of the more recent species to be defined, having been defined in 2002 (Brunet et al. 2002). But ideas about our past extend to the beginnings of recorded history.

Across several disciplines there has been a long debate about the makeup of human nature (see Willoughby 2005). At some point in our past we were nonhuman animals. When did we start to change, and why? Three features are generally considered to mark the transition from the nonhuman to the human: bipedalism (the ability to walk upright); brain size; and the initiation of stone technology.

Bipedalism

There are at least twelve distinct hypotheses as to how and why bipedalism evolved in humans and also some debate as to when it first surfaced. *Homo erectus*—the upright person—has long been considered as the first of our species to walk upright—about two million years ago. In the late 1970s, Mary Leakey discovered a set of footprints in Laetoli (North West Tanzania) that scientists have dated to 3.7 million years ago, almost doubling the earlier date for humans walking upright. In the early years of the twenty-first century, detailed examination of the Toumai skull indicated that our oldest known ancestor—some seven million years ago—walked upright, a quantum leap in paleoanthropology.

---

radioactive decay of isotopes in volcanic deposits above or below the fossil bearing layers (Deino et al. 1998).

At the present time there is no consensus on this matter. The ability to walk upright is still considered to be central evidence for what defines the human beyond other primates. All we can conclude is that the "human as human" has been around much longer than we initially thought. And throughout those several thousands of years—possibly up to seven million years ago—we used our walking capacity to explore our world, with a range of ecological affiliations that progressively became entwined with our evolving psyche, individually and collectively. This feature alone suggests that eco-spirituality may well have been a central features of our lived experience going back into deep time, irrespective of how consciously aware we might have been of its impact on our lives and values.

Brain Size

Compared to the chimpanzee, the human brain is larger, and certain brain regions have been particularly altered during human evolution. Most brain growth of chimpanzees happens before birth, while the development of the human brain happens after birth. As early humans faced new environmental challenges and evolved bigger bodies, they evolved larger and more complex brains. Over the course of human evolution, brain size tripled. The modern human brain is the largest and most complex of any living primate.[5]

Size, however, is not the central issue here. Large, complex brains like ours can process and store a lot of information.

---

[5] Measurements of cranial capacity are rather crude indicators, but they are all that we have. Anatomical studies of *H. erectus* crania suggest much lesser cranial capacity (850–1290 cm^3) than those of Upper Paleolithic *H. sapiens* (1302–1600 cm^3).

That was a big advantage to early humans in their social interactions and encounters with unfamiliar habitats. Such brain capacity enabled humans to engage their environment in ways that were significantly different from our primate ancestors, and that is what is at stake in using brain size as a measuring device for human uniqueness.

In terms of eco-spirituality, our growing awareness of the integral sacredness of life at large belongs not just to the brain but to the mind. The mind is understood today not merely in terms of mental capacity, but of the deeper intuitive wisdom with which we humans engage uniquely with all of life's challenges (Rohr and Boland 2021).

Stone Technology

When we began to use the human mind—imaginatively, intuitively, symbolically—has long been regarded as a post-language development, dating back to some 100,000 years ago. New evidence from ancient stonework garnered throughout the opening years of the twenty-first century indicates an employment of the human mind that stretches us back into deep time, far outstretching the evolution of spoken language. The creation of an Acheulian biface (a hand axe worked on both sides) by *H. erectus* in East Africa (and some time after 600,000 years ago by *H. heidelbergensis*) involved, first, the choice of a stone with a correctly curved surface, followed by a series of actions that followed a defined set of instructions—a "virtual manual," memorized by demonstration and repetition. The instructions involved the formation of separate planes along different axes, minimizing the computational complexities required to create the three-dimensional finished product. There was some skill and intelligence at work here!

Acheulian stonework first appears in the archeological record as early as 1.7 million years ago in the West Turkana area of Kenya and, contemporaneously, in southern Africa. The earliest known Oldowan tools are dated at 2.6 million years ago and were uncovered at Gona in Ethiopia. After this date the Oldowan industry subsequently spread throughout much of Africa. In May 2015, the discovery of 3.3–million-year-old stone tools from the Lomekwi 3 site in Kenya was announced, pushing back the origin of stone toolmaking by 700,000 years. These fossils have not been assigned to a particular species of early *Homo*, but it is now widely accepted that they are the earliest fossils of our genus. In all probability further discoveries await our pursuit of such ingenuity and creativity.

In terms of eco-spirituality, creative stonework carries a double significance. At a very practical level it signals the human yearning to engage with life, using the instruments of nature to connect more intimately with the natural world. Second, it signals the creative urge and the earliest intimations of an artistic flair. These intuitions require us to ask: What Spirit is inspiring such an urge?

Liberating the Spirit of Time

Most if not all the inherited myths of origin are far too shortsighted and time restricted. They are also theologically and spiritually bankrupt when taken literally. They present a God-image based on human projections at a time when it seems our species was undergoing a confused—and confusing—transition from hunter-gatherer status to that of patriarchal land managers—between approximately 10,000 and 5000 BCE. The Hebrew scriptures offer a valuable overview of that turbulent development.

The Book of Genesis begins with the creative narrative of the Spirit drawing forth new lifeforms from the living organicity of the earth itself. Throughout, we are reminded that "God saw that it was good." The plot begins to go awry when humans seek to dominate the scene, with the patriarchal male seeking to control all. The more he tries, the more everything falls out of control, so that, by the end of the Book of Genesis, the violent imperial male is deeply immersed in the strategy of conquer and control, with the patriarchal God nearly always supporting the violent conqueror.

Historian Karen Armstrong offers this bleak and dis-turbing resume:

> By the end of Chapter Three, Yahweh has completely lost control of his creation, and the fair-minded, im-partial God is guilty of monstrous favouritism. We are made to feel the pain of those whom he quite arbitrarily and cruelly rejects—Cain, Esau, Hagar and Ishmael. The kindly Creator God becomes a cruel destroyer during the Flood, when, in a fit of pique, he eliminates almost the entire human species. (Armstrong 2019, 92).

As the Hebrew scriptures unfold, patriarchal violence be-comes entwined in the institution of kingship, postulated on the conviction that the God who rules the world is himself a king, reigning and ruling from a heavenly throne above and beyond this perverse vale of tears. Since the divine kingship from on high never seems to master the deviant situation, eventually the ruling God decides to send his own Son (in human form) to mediate and facilitate a more enduring resolution. However, the violence of deviant humans continues long after the Jesus event, indeed, right down to our own time.

How can we ever hope to get things back on track? First, can we begin at least to acknowledge the fact that our authentic God-endowed human story is not one of a mere few thousand years (whether two thousand, five thousand, or even ten thousand), but one of seven million years. Can we begin to come to terms with the fact that our God has been working in and through us throughout that entire time?

The Creative Imperative

The problematic nature of the human condition seems to be an unquestioned assumption for different religious traditions around the globe. No other starting point is acceptable. Immediately, this casts the divine power (we name God) into a rescuing role, and despite the alleged almighty power of this God, the ruling deity seems unable to resolve the sin-laden dilemma. Codependent religiosity reigns supreme and has become so normalized that nobody within the religions seems to know how to engage its underlying corruption.

To address this dilemma, some try to rectify the problematic elements of our inherited religions. As a social scientist, I have serious reservations about this strategy. I am prepared to accept the argument that religion has been a force for good, but it has been so always at a big price and in a congested package that misses so much of the elegant grandeur of the alternative narrative I am exploring in the present work.

Eco-spirituality offers a very different starting point. It opts for deep time and an expanded space horizon. It embraces the evolving vision of *creatio ex profundis* (creation out of chaos) rather than the patriarchal construct of *creatio ex nihilo*. It works on a basic assumption that God's creativity is operative throughout creation at every stage of our long evolutionary story, at the cosmic, planetary, and human levels alike. There has never been a time in which that creativity was not at work. In each new evolutionary emergence, there is a genuine novelty around which the Holy One rejoices, affirms, and celebrates.

Consequently, seven million years ago, when the new species called humans first evolved on earth, God was doing a new thing: "Behold I make all things new" (Rev 21:5). The co-creative God of that new original moment was not looking down the timeline and surmising "I will now co-create these new creatures called humans, but I know they'll mess things up, and I have another plot to sort that out, and when that will have been done (through Jesus, my beloved Son), then I will declare humans to be saved." This line of argument has nothing to do with God, but, as indicated previously, arises from a set of patriarchal projections from a distorted and confused stage of our human evolutionary story, largely influenced by the formal rise of agriculture about ten thousand years ago. As we moved to the rational management of land and its resources, we seem to have lost the inherited ancient creativity that had sustained us for several thousand years.

"If we want to tackle the greatest challenges of our times—from climate crisis to our growing distrust of one another—then I think the place we need to start is our view of human nature" (Rutger Bregman 2020, 9). For many theorists even to this day, however, this starting point tends to be negatively and problematically moralistic. Consider another starting point, proposed by anthropologist Agustin Fuentes Fuentes (2017) and beautifully summarized by science journalist Simon A. Worrall in *National Geographic* (April 23, 2017):

> We tend to think of these beautiful cave paintings of the big mastodons and wild oryx as art. But that's only about 40,000 years old. We know that 85,000 years ago, in southern Africa, our ancestors were carving on ostrich eggshells. Twenty thousand years earlier than that, they were drilling holes in small shells and wearing them around their necks. One hundred thousand years before that, they were crumbling ochre and rubbing it on their bodies. Five hundred thousand years before that, half a million years ago, they were making tools that were incredibly beautiful and more symmetrical and aesthetic than they had to be to do their jobs. Art is very deep in human history.

Systems theorist Jeremy Lent takes us even deeper into ancient resourcefulness, suggesting that, for much of our evolutionary story, we cooperated with a pre-human patterning instinct inherent to organic life at large:

> Our patterning instinct honed over millions of years to find meaning in the complex experience of daily life, plays a crucial role in the drive to imbue our own mental characteristics into the world around us. In prelinguistic times, its powers helped early humans successfully navigate their increasingly sophisticated communities. With the emergence of language, it drove infants to impute meaning into the cacophony of sounds with which they were bombarded. With its unrelenting compulsion for patterning, its prowess

was then applied to look for meaning in the otherwise seemingly chaotic occurrences of the universe. (Lent 2017, 76)[6]

This alternative view of human nature, endowed with an ancient capacity for creativity and cooperation, must now be embraced as a more credible and authentic description of our evolving human story. Consequently, three important features need to be kept in mind here—central to the unfolding wisdom of eco-spirituality:

1. There was never an idyllic age in which humans were perfect and got everything right, as if they were angels or some kind of superior, godlike beings. Such a portrayal makes no evolutionary sense, and worse still, it seriously undermines the foundational creativity that has sustained and enhanced human evolution over several thousand years.

2. Struggle, a quality of engagement with trial and error, is consistently the modus operandi of our species over the long stretch of evolutionary becoming. There is evidence to suggest that we learned as we went along and got it right for much of the time. Our deep capacity for creativity is what has kept us on course.[7]

---

[6] Beyond the human level, we note that German mathematician Emmy Noether (1882–1935) highlighted a patterning process throughout creation, a claim which mainline science only formally recognized in the latter half of the twentieth century; for more, see Clegg 2021.

[7] In the words of Agustin Fuentes: "The cooperative and creative responses to the conflicts the world throws at us, and those we create ourselves, reshape the world around us, which in turn reshapes

3. Whereas the post-agricultural era, approximately the past ten thousand years, is characterized by violence, exploitation (including of land), and, often fierce competition, our default position throughout the epoch of deep time is that of cooperation and collaboration. The human brain (and psyche) is programmed primarily for cooperation and not for competition, an understanding that modern education at all life-stages has neither acknowledged nor appropriated responsibly (see Rifkin 2009).

Today, the oldest date we have for such foundational creativity is 3.3 million years ago. The evidence usually cited for ancient human creativity is that of Ice Age art and the famous caves of Lascaux and Chauvet in France, Swabian Jura in Germany, and El Castillo in Spain. This covers a time span of about ten thousand years between thirty thousand and forty thousand years ago. In Australia and Africa we have evidence for similar artistic expression pointing back 100,000 years and further.

The significance of Ice Age art has been keenly researched for over one-hundred years now, and several explanations have been offered. Today, David Lewis-Williams (2002) is one widely recognized authority who favors the interpretation of such art being the result of trance-like states, mediated by a shaman, with the cave itself serving as a symbolic space between this creation and the spirit world. To describe them as sites of ancient worship is appropriate but not to be confused with religious worship as we know it today.

---

our bodies and minds. We are the species that has a hand in making itself—niche constructors extraordinaire" (Fuentes 2017, 10). For more on our adeptness at "niche switching," see Heying and Weinstein 2021, 10–11, 35–36.

In the twenty-first century we encounter a double hurdle that eco-spirituality must negotiate. First, such ancient art expresses unique creative potential, but second, and perhaps more difficult to accept, we evidence a strong mystical dimension that ardent religionists will dismiss as primitive paganism (animism) and anti-religionists will use to reinforce their view that all religion has primitive roots. Up to a few thousand years ago, across the entire human world, it seems there was no dualistic split between the sacred and the secular. An underlying oneness was assumed, enriched by an amorphous sense of divine empowerment, mediated through several God-images (polytheism)[8] and experientially known through a range of ritualistic behaviors. The dualistic splitting we moderns take so much for granted, and the pernicious ideologies that have evolved in the name of (monotheistic) religions, blind and prejudice us from being able to see or understand this alternative way of being in the world.

Returning to our underlying creative streak, Ice Age art provides an initial compelling and inspiring insight. Until the mid-twentieth century, Ice Age art was as far back as we could trace evidence for human creativity—approximately forty thousand years ago. As the study of human origins (paleontology) quickly advanced from about 1980 onward, so too did the evidence for the human capacity for creativity and innovation.

The focus moved from art to stonework, and from Europe to Africa. In 1949, British physical anthropologist

---

[8] Whereas in our time, polytheism tends to be equated with the pagan worship of false gods, even as recently as early Christian times, it denoted a sense of divine multiplicity, within which a range of engagements with the Divine was both accepted and accommodated (see Asla 2017; Ehrman 2018).

Kenneth P. Oakley (d. 1981) published a short book entitled *Man the Tool-Maker* (Oakley 1949). Based on what many today consider limited research, it nonetheless evoked a scholarly curiosity that led to the unearthing of human potentialities largely unknown until that time, but that are now foundational to understanding the creativity being explored in the present work. While much of the scholarly interest focuses on the functional value of such ancient stone tools—for digging, scraping, and especially for extracting meat from animal bones—there has been an enduring curiosity on possible underlying artistic motifs. For instance, Oakely describes a dark-red jasperite pebble found at a South African archeological site (Makapansgat Member 4) dated to around three million years ago. The pebble has a shape that is reminiscent of a humanoid face and was transported far from its site of origin, suggesting that it was valued by the (probably) ancient ancestor who found it, perhaps because of its suggestive human likeness.

Gowlett (1984, 2011) has discussed the necessity of the Acheulian toolmaker to see the outline of the tool "in the mind's eye" or to use a "visuospatial sketchpad." Creating an Acheulian biface, as noted above, involved use of the human imagination, coordinating manual skill with perceptual acuity and a level of intelligence unique for that time. To say the least, it leaves the primitive hypothesis lacking!

The study of ancient stone technology made significant strides in the second decade of the twenty-first century, focusing largely on functional (as distinct from artistic) use. In 2010, a startling announcement was made: two bones with stone-tool butchery marks dated at 2.6 million years ago had been found at the Dikika site in Ethiopia, pushing the earliest traces of meat eating nearly a million years earlier than previously known. This was also far earlier than the earliest *Homo* fossils. Does this mean *Australopithecus* (the proto-human) was just picking up naturally sharp rocks to use as stone knives (as most researchers claim), or was it something of a more sophisticated, imaginative set of skills with possible artistic intent?

Scientific research continues to delve deeper for possible creative breakthroughs. The announcement about stone tools from the Lomekwi 3 site in Kenya, mentioned above, occurred in May 2015, just two months after a 2.8-million-year-old fossil mandible and teeth were uncovered from the Ledi-Geraru research area in Ethiopia. The jaw predates the previously known fossils of the *Homo* lineage by approximately 400,000 years. These are the earliest known fossils in our ancestral genus, and they will not be the last to be uncovered.

In April 2016, *Scientific American* carried a lead story on the pioneering work of Dietrich Stout, professor of anthropology at Emory University in Atlanta, Georgia. Seeking to replicate the stone-technology behavior of our ancient ancestors, Stout has set up a pioneering project, working collaboratively with a team of neuroscientists to detect brain activity during prolonged sessions of stone "knapping" (see Stout 2016). Consistently, the brain activity being recorded and observed evidences high levels of creativity.

The Artistic Flair

This pioneering endeavor challenges and even undermines the long-held view among language researchers that human creativity, including intelligence, imagination, and intuition, was only possible after language evolved, approximately 100,000 years ago. It has long been assumed that prior to that time humans were no better than animals in our ability to perceive and comprehend. In their argument the ingredients of human intelligence fall into place after language, and humans slowly evolve the capacity to engage their environment in more intelligently informed ways. This view could be described as *the restrictive language hypothesis.*

Ever since Kenneth Oakley's suggestion that our ancient toolmakers were endowed with an intelligent—and even artistic—flair, the restrictive language hypothesis is no longer defensible. Neuro-anthropologist Terence Deacon indicates that language does not mark the beginning of more advanced human intelligibility, incorporating human creativity and a capacity for symbolism (Deacon 1997). Rather, language is the outcome of a species that has been portraying such creativity over several thousand years, thus co-creating the critical evolutionary threshold that leads to language as we understand it today.

To date, the oldest evidence for our human artistic flair tends to be traced to Lower Paleolithic times. Two discoveries are frequently cited: the Venus of Berekhat Ram (c. 230,000–700,000 BCE) and the Venus of Tan-Tan (c. 300,000–500,000 BCE). These are generally considered to be the products of our Neanderthal ancestors. Also of interest to researchers are the Bhimbetka Petroglyphs, ten cupules and a groove, discovered in the quartzite auditorium rock shelter at Bhimbetka in Madhya Pradesh, central India, dating to at least 290,000 BCE.

Human creativity is much older and more insinuated into our evolutionary flourishing than we have ever suspected. It is the long-repressed truth that now needs to be reclaimed in an anthropological narrative and spiritual synthesis that must overcome the primitive assumptions to which science and religion have been wedded for far too long. Fortunately, more rigorous science itself invites us to such daring new horizons. Scholar of comparative studies Christopher Collins explores the cognitive skills that predate language and writing (Collins 2013). These include the brain's capacity to perceive the visible world, store its images, and retrieve them later to form simulated mental events. Long before humans could share stories through articulate speech, they perceived, remembered, and imagined their world in a range of preverbal narratives.

As indicated above, since May 2015 the oldest dating for ancient stone technology is about 3.3 million years ago. We can no longer assume that this was merely a functional endeavor, serving only rational and pragmatic purposes. Although we have no concrete evidence for an artistic dimension to date, the research of Dietrich Stout and others requires us to keep open the possibility—even the likelihood—that in time such evidence will be forthcoming. In our species the capacity for creativity seems considerably older than we currently assume.

In the construction of eco-spirituality, we need to begin with that ancient underlying creativity rather than with the flawed human nature upon which so much formal religion is postulated. Let us not be accused of living in a falsely utopian world, in denial of our sinful nature and the havoc we have always reaped because of our immoral recklessness. This negative anthropology reflects well the contemporary landscape now described as the epoch of the Anthropocene. As indicated previously, it describes quite well human behavior of the past ten thousand years, but not before then. Furthermore, it is no longer culturally or religiously responsible to keep projecting onto our ancient ancestors the behaviors of our time that we so much detest.

As creatures of Spirit and not merely of "flesh," our underlying creativity is primary evidence for the Spirit at work within and around us, across several eons of deep time. Any religion that refuses to engage this ancient wisdom short circuits the foundational mystery within which we all breathe, live, and have our being. Such religiosity has outlived its usefulness, and clinging to it is only going to make matters worse for humans and our earth. Eco-spirituality, on the other hand, opts for a deeper analysis of both faith and humanity—or, perhaps, faith in humanity—and calls us all to a more profound discernment of how the creative Spirit of God operates across time and culture.

Critical Issues for Ongoing Discernment

1. The study of human origins largely belongs to the second half of the twentieth century, highlighting the fact that our human species has inhabited the earth for an estimated *seven million years,* and the creativity of God's Spirit has been fully at work in us throughout that entire time.

2. In terms of eco-spirituality, creative stonework (dated now to at least 3.3 million years ago) carries a double significance. It signals the human yearning to engage with life, using the instruments of nature to connect more intimately with the natural world. Second, however, is the creative urge, and the earliest intimations of an artistic flair, energized by the Holy Spirit of God, thus dating spirituality long before formal religions ever evolved.

3. In our long evolutionary story there was no original utopian state in which humans coexisted in harmonic innocence. We learned as we went along, under the lure and guidance of the creative Spirit. And we got it right most of time, because we remained very close to nature, wherein, it seems, the Spirit works most effectively in us and through us.

4. Human creativity is much older and more insinuated into our evolutionary flourishing than we have ever suspected. *It is the long repressed truth that now needs to be reclaimed* in an anthropological narrative and spiritual synthesis that must overcome the

primitive assumptions to which science and religion
have been wedded for far too long.

5. "If we want to tackle the greatest challenges of our
   times—from climate crisis to our growing distrust of
   one another—then I think the place we need to start is
   our view of human nature" (Rutger Bregman 2020, 9).

Overtaken by the World

I do not take the name of God to be the name of a being, of an existent, but of a way I have been overtaken by the world.

—JOHN D. CAPUTO

An Evolutionary must be able to look at the movements of nature, culture, and cosmos as a whole, yet without denying the infinite detail that surrounds us.

—CARTER PHIPPS

In the present chapter I dwell more deeply in that sacred space named in the opening quotation as "the world." Theologian John Caputo suggests that instead of being preoccupied with seeking clarity and truth about the metaphysical qualities of God or with the more individual search for a "personal" relationship with God (or with Jesus), we need to open ourselves up to the God who is forever seeking to reach us—in and through the creation itself.

For billions of years before humans evolved or religions or churches ever came into existence, the energizing creativity of the Great Spirit was at work in the cosmic creation and planetary unfolding of universal life. Our own coming into being—born out of the womb of the creative universe—is beautifully articulated by British scientist Lewis Dartnell:

> I want to explore how the Earth made us. The water in your body once flowed down the Nile, fell as monsoon rain onto India, and swirled around the Pacific. The carbon in the organic molecules of your cells was mined from the atmosphere by the plants that we eat. The salt in your sweat and tears, the calcium of your bones, and iron in your blood all eroded out of the rocks of Earth's crust; and the sulphur of the protein molecules in your hair and muscles was spewed out by volcanoes. The Earth has also provided us with the raw materials we have extracted, refined, and assembled into our tools and technologies, from the roughly fashioned hand-axes of the Stone Age, to today's computers and smart phones. These planetary influences drove our evolution in East Africa as a uniquely intelligent, communicative, and resourceful kind of creature. (Dartnell 2019, 1)

Life as Gift

In Chapter 1, I introduced the notion of life as gift, and I now extend that gifted horizon in terms of Caputo's insight that we inhabit a world by which we have been overtaken. First, note the concluding sentence of the quote from Lewis Dartnell: "a uniquely intelligent, communicative, and resourceful kind of creature." This image of the human is so very different from the inherited Christian emphasis on original sin and our flawed condition. We are overtaken, not by a flawed, deranged world, but by one in which everything is to be viewed and treated as gift. This is, indeed, countercultural, almost to the point of sheer exaggeration.

Throughout our long human story, the give and take of gifts in everyday life creates, maintains, and strengthens various social bonds—cooperative, competitive, or antagonistic—that in turn, define personal identities and our ways of relating to the world at large. Examining the gift and the gift economy, therefore, provides us with an effective and unique means of understanding the formation of personhood and the structure of social relations over many eons.[1]

We are ones who gift—except for one painful exception, namely, the capitalistic monetary system adopted across the modern world! Capitalism operates on the basis of one massively flawed assumption, namely, that the goods of creation are scarce.[2] That being the case, we need structures to compete for the scarce goods and turn to another rendition of natural selection (Charles Darwin) or the survival of the fittest (Herbert Spencer). Truthfully, however, we inhabit a creation of *abundance*, not one of scarcity. Abundance is our default position, but social and economic theories originating in the aftermath of Britain's Industrial Revolution created an ideology of scarcity that haunts our world to our own time.

---

[1] Among the leading names that have studied the cultural significance of gifting, French sociologist Marcel Mauss, in his 1925 essay "The Gift," is a pioneering source. His seminal work has also influenced philosophers, artists, and political activists, including Georges Bataille, Jacques Derrida, Jean Baudrillard, and more recently David Graeber as well as theologians John Milbank, Jean-Luc Marion, and Marshall Sahlins.

[2] Although it can be traced back to Adam Smith, the notion of scarcity as foundational to our understanding of capitalism was largely developed by British economist Lionel Robbins (d. 1984).

Briefly, the historical context belongs primarily to Thomas Malthus (1766–1834), cleric, historian, and economist who, in his 1798 "An Essay on the Principle of Population," describes the outcome of humankind's struggle to obtain increasingly limited resources within a life filled with misery and vice. Malthus believed that the inability of available resources to keep pace with ever increasing population size ultimately results in a continuing struggle for survival by the lower economic classes. This concept of a struggle for survival within large populations was adopted by evolutionary biologists, most notably by Charles Darwin.

Malthus was heavily influenced by the changes wrought by the Industrial Revolution, which radically transformed the economic structure of British society from a system of feudalism—a hierarchical system of lords and serfs that concentrated wealth at the top—to one of capitalism. Free enterprise and cost-efficient machines enabled factory owners, bankers, and entrepreneurs to gain significant wealth and power. The middle and upper classes prospered from the labors of the poor, who filled the factories and toiled long hours for little pay.

In the ensuing capitalistically influenced understanding of life, the very notion of gifting was severely undermined by the exclusive focus on people and human need. *Anthropocentrism* (prioritizing the human over all other life forms—and over creation as well) dictated all other values, and the prevailing Christian religion of the time, largely preoccupied with the salvation of the human soul, reinforced the exclusive focus on human beings and their capacity for making money from the goods (not the gifts) of creation.

Despite the economic fallacy outlined above, scholars of the humanities and social sciences alike have joined forces to explore the dynamic, complex world of gifts from different disciplinary perspectives and approaches, such as literature, philosophy, sociology, law, economics, and marketing research (see Cheal 1988; Hyland 2009; Satlow 2013). The growing literature also shows that, as the human interest in and capacity for doing gift exchange are consistently changing in response to a rapidly shifting environment of social life at large, the enigmatic gift will likely remain an attractive subject in anthropology and beyond.

Gifting as a Cosmic Endowment

Eco-spirituality, however, requires us to move into a more expansive horizon whereby the notion of gifting needs to be understood not merely as a human phenomenon but as a central feature of all creation. In the words of naturalist David Suzuki:

> The way we see the world shapes the way we treat it. If a mountain is a deity, not a pile of ore; if a river is one of the veins of the land, not potential irrigation water; if a forest is a sacred grove, not timber; if other species are biological kin, not resources; or if the planet is our mother, not an opportunity—then we will treat each other with greater respect. Thus is the challenge, to look at the world from a different perspective.[3]

Those of us who have the privilege of living amid nature, whether in countryside or city, will know something of the enrichment of the natural world in our own lives and how

---

[3] I have not been able to locate the source of this frequently cited reference.

this rich resourcefulness contributes daily to the growth and development of other organisms as well.

On the still larger scale of cosmic life, we can take the sun as an example of this gratuitous gifting. The sun burns by transforming hydrogen into helium at fantastic explosive temperatures. In producing its heat and light, it burns up four million tons of itself every second. At any moment the sun emits about 3.86×10^{26} watts of energy. So, add 24 zeros to 386, and you'll get an idea of how unimaginably large an amount of energy that is! Most of that energy goes off into space, but about 1.74×10^{17} watts strike the earth. Earth is bathed in huge amounts of energy from the sun—885 million terawatt hours every year. This is a lot—around sixty-two hundred times the amount of commercial primary energy used in the world in any one year.

British philosopher Toby Ord observes:

> Our Solar System's greatest contribution to our potential lies with our Sun, and the vast bounty of clean energy it offers. The sunlight hitting earth's surface each day carries 5,000 times more energy than modern civilization requires. It gives in two hours what we use in a year. This abundance of solar energy created most of our other energy sources (coal, oil, natural gas, wind, hydro, biomass) and far outstrips them. (Ord 2020, 227–28)

Over several millennia our ancient ancestors worshiped the sun. Intuitively and instinctively, for people over many eons, the sun served as a living icon for the energizing empowerment of the Great Spirit. From the sun originates all the chemical ingredients involved in the process of photosynthesis, conveying sheer aliveness into all organic life, and nourishing humans every day through the gift of daily food.

However, that is not where our human story begins. We have to travel further back into deep time and gaze to the stars, where the life of each human originates. American naturalist Melanie Challenger vividly articulates:

> We and the Earth and all its other life forms are made of the shrapnel of a dead star. By the time we reach adulthood, our bodies hold within them more than sixty elements, the residue of this primal kind of extinction. We are a sheaf of empty space and ancient electricity, an unimaginable quantity of atoms, carrying protons and neutrons and somersaulting electrons. Our bodies are the sum of many trillions of cells, a proportion of which renew themselves multiple times throughout our life. We are the billions of letters of a genome and a whole fizzing microbial community of bacteria, yeasts, viruses and helminth parasites such as round worms and tape worms. Assuming no impediment, we are a primate with a brain, possessing vast quantities of nerve cells linked together into a large complex. . . . Like all other life on earth, we are the offspring of shared processes, a confederacy of matter that can metamorphose into the seemingly limitless wonders of life. (Challenger 2021, 200–201)

With these reflections we glimpse something of the deeper meaning Caputo has in mind when he describes God as "a way I have been overtaken by the world" (Caputo 2015, 179).

Long before we employed metaphysical categories to explain the meaning of God, and God's role in our lives, humans apprehended the mysterious animation of God's

Spirit at work in the evolving processes of the natural world. This is where eco-spirituality wants to begin the exploration into God and God's desire for our world and for all its creatures. In and through the creation—in all its cosmic and planetary elegance—we get our first and deepest insight into the reality we call God. And the God of that encounter, as reviewed in Chapter 2 above, is what several Indigenous Peoples describe as the Great Spirit.

Ecology and Bioregionalism

Ecology came to the attention of the general public in the 1960s, when environmental issues were rising to the forefront of our global consciousness. Although scientists have been studying the natural world for centuries, ecology in the modern sense is a development of the late nineteenth century.[4] Around this time European and American scientists began studying how plants function and their effects on the habitats around them. Eventually this led to the study of how animals interact with plants and other animals, shaping the ecosystems in which they live. In 1962, marine biologist and ecologist Rachel Carson's book Silent Spring helped to mobilize the environmental movement by alerting the public to the effects of toxic pesticides (such as DDT) in the environment. Carson used ecological science to link the release of environmental toxins and their consequent impact on human health and ecosystemic well-being. Since then, ecologists have worked to bridge their understanding of the degradation of the planet's

---

[4] The word *ecology* was coined in 1866 by German zoologist Ernst Haeckel (d. 1919), who applied the term *oekologie* to the relation of the animal both to its organic as well as its inorganic environment.

ecosystems with environmental politics, law, restoration, and natural-resource management.

Ecology is necessarily the union of many areas of study because its definition is all-encompassing. The largest scale of ecological organization is the biosphere: the total sum of ecosystems on the planet. Ecosystems are complex adaptive systems where the interaction of life processes form self-organizing patterns across different scales of time and space. An ecosystem is a geographic area where plants, animals, and other organisms, as well as weather and landscape, work together to form a bubble of life. Ecosystems contain living (biotic) parts as well as nonliving (abiotic) parts.[5]

Ecosystems can be very large or very small. The whole surface of earth is a series of connected ecosystems. Ecosystems are often connected in a larger biome. Biomes are large sections of land, sea, or atmosphere. Forests, ponds, reefs, and tundra are all types of biomes, for example. They're organized very generally based on the types of plants and animals that live in them. Within each forest, each pond, each reef, or each section of tundra, there are many different ecosystems.

The notion of the bioregion and our human engagement with it is foundational to our human engagement with ecology and with the spiritual challenges of the present work. In scientific terms bioregionalism denotes an area constituting a natural ecological community with characteristic flora, fauna, and environmental conditions and bounded by natural rather than artificial borders. The geologian Thomas Berry further elaborates:

---

[5] Biotic factors include plants, animals, and other organisms. Abiotic factors include rocks, temperature, and humidity.

A bioregion is an identifiable geographic area of interacting life-systems that is relatively self-sustaining in the
ever-renewing process of nature. The full diversity of
life functions is carried out, not as individuals, or as a
species, but as a community that includes the physical,
as well as the organic components of a region. Such a
bioregion is self-propagating, self-nourishing, self-edu-
cating, self-governing, self-healing, and a self-fulfilling
community. Each of the component life-systems must
integrate its own functioning within this community
to survive in an effective manner. (Berry 1985, 166)[6]

In a workshop for a group of missionaries we were each
required to complete a questionnaire about our bioregion.
Its twenty questions asked about the sources of our daily
food; the grasses, plants, and animals inhabiting a particular locality; recycling of waste products; local methods of
agriculture; and so on. In terms of my childhood home in
rural Ireland I could answer seventeen of the twenty questions. At the time, however, I had been living in London
for over five years. In terms of my London location, I could
only answer five of the twenty questions.

The point of the exercise was to establish how well we
knew our local bioregions. At the time, I was not even sure
what the concept of bioregionalism meant. The exercise

---

[6] The roots of bioregionalism go back to the 1930s when Fredric
Clements and Victor Shelford developed the biome system of clas-
sification. Biomes refer to natural habitats such as grasslands, deserts,
rainforests, and coniferous forests shaped by climate. Particular soils,
vegetation, and animal life develop in each climate region in accordance with rainfall, temperature, and weather patterns. The state of
California, for example, constitutes ten major bioregions; the great
plains of the Midwest comprises three bioregions.

clearly indicated that, in terms of my London home, I was poorly grounded in my bioregion, whereas, in my childhood home of rural Ireland, I was intimately interconnected with the surrounding environment.

Born into a poor Irish family in the late 1940s, life was quite a struggle, and yet, like most families around us, we were largely self-sufficient. We had four cows that gave us milk and cream, thirty hens producing eggs and young chicks that my mother sold at the local market, and a pig. We grew a few acres of wheat, which was crushed into flour at the local mill. From that, my mother baked all the bread we consumed. Once a year we grew a potato crop, our staple diet for a whole year, and once a year we killed a pig, providing the meat for the entire family. Some of our neighbors had sheep, from whose wool a woman in the local village spun the yarn for our sweaters and socks. And, from the local piece of bog-land, we obtained the turf to keep the home fire aflame. That fire was not merely a source of heat and comfort in cold weather, but it was the base for all heating and cooking.

Against that background, I knew my bioregion intimately and many years before I began to understand the ecological niche that provided both my basic human needs and a deeply intimate grounding from which I could understand the sacredness of the natural world. The creativity and generosity of God's unconditional love had seeped into my inner being, a (super)natural integration I only became aware of several years later.

The Bioregional Basis of Faith

Acquaintance with one's bioregion is one of the most effective ways of engaging with our earthiness as a human species. Therein we know the interdependent immediacy whereby our human life, and that of all the other co-partners in the bioregion, is of one and the same essence. This earth intimacy is also the realm where the Great Spirit awakens the kind of sensitivity so foundational to the development of eco-spirituality. In my own awakening to the significance of the bioregion, I penned these words in a previous work:

> Intuitively I know the call of the early dawn, and the balm of a crimson sunset. I relish the wind's energy blowing in my face as I roam beloved mountains or lie still on the grass of the meadows I cherished as a child. I feel an affinity with the stately oak trees, while the emergence of the first snowdrops evoke my tender care. As I hold a handful of uncontaminated soil, I realize I am gazing into the depths of my own soul. (O'Murchu 2022, 93)

Might that be the same friendly coexistence our human species have known throughout much of our long evolutionary story, long before formal religions ever came to be? Deeply immersed in the organicity of the living earth, did we not have firsthand experience of our earth belonging, along with the creativity of the Great Spirit at work in our lives? Truthfully, the current adversarial attitude toward the earth and its creatures is a development of merely the past few thousand years.

Today, most people live in cities, often amid sprawling conditions of poverty and ecological deprivation. Connection with the natural world is severely limited, and acquaintance with bioregional grounding is about as remote as one could imagine. Even for many people living in rural areas, life has become so commodified—for example, we buy all our food rather than grow it ourselves—that conscious immersion in our bioregions is quite rare. Some of the best examples of bioregional interconnection come to us from the Indigenous Peoples of the world.

Nonetheless, this is not merely an item of peripheral interest for eco-spirituality. It is of central importance to the entire vision and scope of what is involved. Ecology enriches our world and is crucial for human well-being and prosperity at every level. It provides new knowledge of the interdependence between people and nature that is vital for food production, maintaining clean air and water, and sustaining biodiversity in a changing climate, and also for the ethical and moral values so urgently needed for the well-being of all creatures on earth today.

This ecological context is not merely a new insight for spirituality in the twenty-first century. It is a central feature of our Christian faith. Maintaining a mosaic of habitats, bioregionalism is central to the biblical notion of the *oikos*, a Greek word denoting house, home, and household with a distinctive organic communal meaning. This is illustrated by biblical scholar Michael Crosby, who writes, "In the Mediterranean world of Jesus, the house was not so much the building itself, but the ordering of relationships taking place within it among persons and their resources" (Crosby 2012, 100).

This brief biblical description indicates that the building itself (house/home) is the harbinger for the development of empowering relationships among the immediate family and with all living organisms constituting the wider web of life (which is precisely what the bioregion denotes). Consequently, creation at large may be described as *the household of God*, a term used extensively by the biblical scholar John Dominic Crossan, to denote God's own presence in the unfolding process of creation at large.

Consequently, when Crossan writes that "we are as human beings co-responsible with the Householder for the household of the world," we are identifying a new understanding of God, one more congruent with, and relevant for, the emerging vision of eco-spirituality (Crossan 2010, 50). Contrary to the human-centered spirituality of earlier times, eco-spirituality's focus is not on the priority of humans and less so on the salvation of the human soul. Eco-spirituality focuses on a new interactive engagement with God as householder and with all creatures as participants in the well-being and development of the bioregional household. This commitment is not about transcending the vale of tears in favor of a heavenly realm hereafter or about wiping away the tears from every human eye. Eco-spirituality is about the transformation of the whole creation to support and advance its organic evolution.

The Invitation to Go Deeper

In the 1970s, environmentalist Arne Naess introduced the notion of *deep ecology*, a term suggesting that environmentalism, in its strongest incarnation, must have a fundamental change in the way humanity defines itself as part of nature at its root.[7] Deep ecology seeks to promote a human lifestyle based on a closer harmony with nature through stronger bioregional grounding. Deep ecology recognizes diverse communities of life on earth that are

---

[7] It is described as "deep" because it is regarded as looking more deeply into the reality of humanity's relationship with the natural world, arriving at philosophically more profound conclusions than those of mainstream environmentalism.

composed through biotic factors and, where applicable, through ethical relations, that is, the valuing of other beings as more than just resources.

Deep ecology already embodies what eco-spirituality seeks to make more explicit. That transition, however, is neither smooth nor linear, and, as reviewed by the historian Neil MacGregor (2018), can only be negotiated when we first understand the impact of formal religion over several centuries. Thus, Arne Naess (1976) criticized the Christian tradition, stating that the Bible supports an anthropocentric arrogance whereby we, humans, predicate ourselves as God's designated managers of all organic life.

The critic most often cited in this regard is former UCLA professor of medieval science and technology Lynn White Jr. (d. 1987), who suggests that the main reason why the West has so carelessly abused the natural world is because of its grounding in traditional Christian values, according to which God made man in his own image and gave him dominion over the earth. In other words, nature has no value apart from what it provides for us, and thus we are free to exploit it without consequence.

Christianity has become ever more aware of this dilemma and has made various attempts to transcend the dualistic split between earth and spirit. Between 1996 and 1998, a three-year international conference series—Religions of the World and Ecology—took place at Harvard University. Over eight hundred scholars gathered to examine the varied ways in which human-earth relations have been conceived in the world's religious traditions. The intention of the series was to assist in establishing a new field of study within religious studies that would link to the interdisciplinary field of environmental studies and have implications for public policy on environmental issues. The series of ten conferences examined the traditions of Judaism, Christianity, Islam, Hinduism, Jainism, Buddhism, Daoism, Confucianism, Shinto, and Indigenous religions.[8] Recognizing that religions are key shapers of people's worldviews and formulators of their most cherished values, this broad research project uncovered a vast wealth of attitudes toward nature sanctioned by religious traditions. In addition, the project identified over one hundred examples of religiously inspired environmental practices and projects in various parts of the world, ranging from reforestation in India and Africa to preservation of herbal knowledge in South America, from the protection of coral reefs in the Pacific regions to the conservation of wildlife in the Middle East.

Befriending Our World amid Climate Change

In the earlier chapters of this book I frequently allude to the prevalence of dualistic splitting so endemic not merely to our inherited faith traditions but to our civilization at

---

[8] The conferences were organized by Mary Evelyn Tucker and John Grim in collaboration with a team of area specialists. The series brought together international scholars of the world's religions, as well as scientists, environmentalists, and grassroots leaders. The papers from these conferences were published in ten volumes by the Center for the Study of World Religions and distributed by Harvard University Press. Three culminating conferences were held at the American Academy of Arts and Sciences in Cambridge, Massachusetts, at the United Nations, and at the American Museum of Natural History. It was at the United Nations press conference that an ongoing Harvard Forum on Religion and Ecology was announced—to continue the research, education, and outreach begun at these earlier conferences. The forum has mounted an international website to assist the field of religion and ecology with introductory papers and annotated bibliographies on the major world religions as well as on science, economy, and policy issues.

large. The external split between earth and heaven, body
and soul, matter and spirit, grace and nature has become
deeply ingrained in the collective psyche of our species, even
amid the growing nonreligious consciousness of our age.
Franciscan theologian Daniel P. Horan describes these splits
well: "One way that climate crisis is a spiritual crisis is that
many Christians compartmentalize their relationship with
God from their relationship to the natural world."[9] Such
compartmentalizing results from something much deeper, so
ingrained in our consciousness, that many among us seem
totally unaware of its impact on our lives, our attitudes, and
our values. The climate emergency of our time provides an
opportunity to wake up to the delusional consciousness we
inhabit, inviting us to other ways of seeing, apprehending,
and understanding the interconnectedness within which all
life evolves and flourishes.

Global climate change is altering every dimension of the
earth's environment. In addition to raising sea levels and
increasing the likelihood of drought and weather-related
natural disasters, climate change is reducing biodiversity,
accelerating energy use, decreasing the planet's volume
of fresh water, reducing the amount of food available for
consumption, and diminishing the natural resources we
need for everything from medicines to building materials.
These alterations in earth's environment are occurring at
an unprecedented rate. Can we bring ourselves to admit
and acknowledge such an impending disaster?

By breaking up people's routines of life, their very liveli-
hoods, their trusted assumptions, and their sense of security,
global climate change confronts human beings with very

---

[9] Daniel P. Horan, "Global Climate Change Is Also a Spiritual
Crisis," *National Catholic Reporter*, July 21, 2021.

serious life questions. Where would I go if climate change
made my home uninhabitable? How would I protect myself
and my family if climate change forced me to move? How
would I secure food and water when everyone around me
is seeking the same thing? What can I plan for the future?
Do I want to bring children into this world? These are just
some of disturbing questions underpinning the eco-anxiety
of our age.

As the 2009 Hindu Declaration on Climate Change
asserts:

> Humanity's very survival depends upon our capacity
> to make a major transition of consciousness, equal
> in significance to earlier transitions from nomadic to
> agricultural, agricultural to industrial, and industrial to
> contemporary technology. We must transit to comple-
> mentarity in place of competition, convergence in place
> of conflict, holism in place of hedonism, optimization
> in place of maximization.[10]

Whether it is the call to engage more deeply with climate
change or with the several other eco-spiritual challenges of
our time, we can no longer deny the basic truth that without
a meaningful earth we earthlings stand little chance of living
with worth and dignity from here on. Let's hope we will
embrace this time of overwhelming crisis as an opportunity
for breakthroughs that will deliver more enduring hope.

---

[10] The 2009 Hindu Declaration on Climate Change, Parliament
of the World's Religions, Melbourne, Australia, December 8, 2009.
An updated declaration was released November 23, 2015.

Critical Issues for Ongoing Discernment

1. While spirituality in its conventional meaning relates to human beings, and to the spiritual life deemed necessary for personal salvation, eco-spirituality begins with creation, the primary revelation of God's unconditional gift of love.
2. It is in and through the creation—in all its cosmic and planetary elegance—that we get our first and deepest insight into the reality we call God.
3. Eco-spirituality requires us to move into a more expansive horizon whereby the notion of gifting needs to be understood not merely as a human phenomenon but as a central feature of all creation.
4. When scripture scholar John D. Crossan writes that "we are as human beings co-responsible with the Householder for the household of the world" (Crossan 2010, 50), we are identifying a new understanding of God, more congruent with, and relevant for, the emerging vision of eco-spirituality.
5. By allowing ourselves to be "overtaken by the world" (Caputo 2015, 179), we stand a better chance of coming home to the sacredness that imbues our world, both within and without.
6. "We are able to understand the nature of creative reality precisely because we, like all life-forms, are part of this reality. We are the world. . . . We express our being in the world by the same means the world forms us." (Weber 2014, 89).

6

Eco-Spirituality:
Creativity and Destruction

The diversity of life that so beguiles us today is the outcome of a long struggle in which organic life keeps breaking through to life forms that are more complex and beautiful. But the cost is terrible. Over thousands of millennia new species arise, thrive, and go extinct. Yes, new life comes from death. But this does not lessen the hard truth that pain and death are woven into the very fabric of life's evolutionary history on earth.

—ELIZABETH JOHNSON

These are questions not only about what kind of life is worth living but what kind of way it's worth dying. . . . At its heart, evolution is about dynamic interactions, not progress.

—MELANIE CHALLENGER

Thanks to the creative insights of contemporary science and our access to them through modern media, millions are now accessing the elegance of creation at an ever deeper level. For many, such information awakens religious-type sentiments at a range of different levels. However, we cannot ignore or bypass the world in peril, which confronts us today no matter where we turn. Any spirituality that tries to dodge that dark and painful side of reality is of little value to either humans or creation at large. It fails to engage the paradox at the heart of creation.

Three issues arise here, each requiring a great deal of discerning wisdom in our time. First, because we now live in an intimately interconnected world, with cyberspace affiliation enabling a sense of global consciousness reaching into the remotest regions of human habitat, we are more conscious than ever of being one global family called to an ever more interactive participation in our own well-being and that of our home planet. In one sense the original dream of the United Nations—co-creating one planetary civilization—seems more tangible than ever.

Despite such advances, we cannot escape the violence and barbarity that humans (and their governments) are imposing upon each other. Poverty, oppression, exploitation (of people and resources), warfare, and fierce competition rage across our world, driving huge sections of humanity to the verge of despair. Despite the massive breakthroughs in interconnectedness, we are still a fractured, disoriented species. Might this be the case because, despite all the religiosity in our world, we still lack an empowering eco-spirituality?

Second, thanks again to the culture of mass information, we are becoming ever more aware of the precarious state of the natural world. As already noted, global warming, caused largely by the burning of fossil fuels that releases carbon dioxide into the atmosphere and creates a greenhouse effect, is emerging as a major threat to several lifeforms on Planet Earth. The cascading consequences include the melting of the polar ice caps, rising sea levels, the release of methane gas trapped in the Siberian tundra, acidification of the oceans, and mass extinctions—all dimensions of a chain reaction becoming ever more difficult to manage or control.

Third, however, an enduring phenomenon of destruction and catastrophe characterizes evolution at every stage of planetary and human unfolding. This is a much more complex issue to wrestle with, but, without engaging it, we cannot hope to address the more immediate ecological and environmental crises in a comprehensive and informed way. Moreover, a meaningful eco-spirituality for the twenty-first century is both incomplete and incoherent without engaging this broader and deeper issue. In previous works (O'Murchu 2008; 2018) I describe it as *the great paradox of Creation-cum-Destruction* (with both concepts carrying equal weight), otherwise named as *the unfolding cycle of birth-death-rebirth*. It is visible all over creation, on the macro and micro scales alike. We cannot escape from it, yet we have somehow managed to dodge and avoid it for several millennia, and most blatantly for the past few thousand years.

Endowed with Paradox

At both the cosmic and planetary levels, we witness this enduring paradoxical mix of newness bursting forth only to yield in due course to decline, fragmentation, and termination.[1] Take, for instance, the stars. Stars burn for billions

---

[1] Philosopher turned economist Charles Eisenstein makes the astute observation that our capitalistic money system is a notable exception to this universal process of birth and death. While everything else in creation wears out and dies, we don't allow this to happen to our money system. Our money has been given an immortal value—similar indeed to a God we worship. Eisenstein claims that we would have a far more dynamic and empowering economic system if we allowed our money to occasionally lose its value, decay, and become redundant (Eisenstein 2011).

of years, constantly making new kinds of atoms. Eventually, these atoms become too big and heavy for this process to continue. When this happens, the inward pressure of gravity overwhelms the outward pressure caused by fusion, and the star implodes. Because every action in physics causes an equal and opposite reaction, the star's implosion results in a dramatic explosion. In that brief moment of tremendous destruction, the light of a single star outshines the entire galaxy. Brilliant, but deadly! We call it a supernova, the death of yet another star.

Out of that deadly hot inferno come the basic building blocks of life, without which we humans, and all other organic creatures, would not even exist. Cosmic destruction is a precondition for so much creativity, life, elegance, and progress. Is this how God created the world? It seems so—to which the average religionist is likely to retort: "How could anyone believe in such a capricious God?" But who is actually capricious, God or us?

Such is the creative paradox at the macro level, characterizing cosmic life across eons that defy human measurement. The same process is at work at the micro level, for instance, within the human microbiome. "Why do microbes so easily slide between pathogen and mutualist?" asks the Malaysian scientific journalist, Ed Yong.

> For a start, these roles are not as contradictory as you might imagine. Think about what a "friendly" gut microbe needs to do to set up a stable relationship with its host. It must survive in the gut, anchor itself so it doesn't get swept away, and interact with its host's cells. These are all things that pathogens must do, too. So both characters—mutualists and pathogens, heroes and villains—often use the same molecules for

the same purposes; they can be used to do wonderful things and terrible things. . . . Every symbiosis is, in its degree, underlain with hostility, and only by proper regulation and often elaborate adjustment can their state of mutual benefit be maintained. (Yong 2016, 82, 83)

Many of us have been heavily indoctrinated by the classical Greek notion of the perfectly omniscient (all-knowing), omnipotent (all-powerful), transcendent (totally independent of all else), immutable (never changing), impassible (beyond suffering), and eternal God, the one who rules and controls everything. Most people don't seem to realize that these divine attributes are actually human *projections* of a species seeking absolute control over everything. The all-powerful deity is actually a projection of power-hungry humans.

Such an understanding of God is little more than five thousand years old and is significantly different from how we related with Holy Mystery for most of our evolutionary story of some seven million years. Our more authentic evolutionary story is much more diverse—and inherently paradoxical. For German philosopher and biologist Andreas Weber, "Every creation is eternally incomplete" (Weber 2014, 102). Therefore, as we open ourselves to being overtaken by God in the world, we will need to learn—and accept—the several contradictory paradoxes that characterize our evolving creation, not merely in terms of today's complexities but, indeed, throughout past eons.

It seems that our ancient ancestors had a very different understanding of the divine life-force, a retrieval that is foundational for the eco-spirituality being explored in the present work. Because of their closeness to the natural world, the ancients, somewhat like contemporary Indigenous

Peoples, knew a convivial relationship with the living universe, experiencing the daily interaction of life and death, creation and destruction, without—it seems—our contemporary compulsion for domination and control.

Take, for instance, the phenomenon of *heterotrophy*. A heterotroph is an organism that cannot produce its own food, instead taking nutrition from other sources of organic carbon, mainly plant or animal matter. In the food chain heterotrophs are primary, secondary, and tertiary consumers, but not producers. In other words, ours is a planet where creatures live off one another, a process that often looks cruel and barbaric to the human eye, oblivious as we are to the fact that we live within a paradoxical creation, of which heterotrophy is a central feature.

Engaging the Power of Paradox

The key word here is *paradox*, which may be described as *a contradiction with meaning written underneath*. On the surface it makes little or no sense, and the imperial Anthropocene has little time for such subtlety. Only the discerning eye (or heart) can perceive the underlying meaning. A familiar example occurs in the writings of St. Paul (see 2 Cor 12:9–11): "When I am weak then I am strong." At a rational level the statement makes no sense, yet many among us can recall life experiences within which the statement rings true. The mystic (of eco-spiritual persuasion), more than anybody else, can entertain and embrace this paradoxical wisdom.

This alternative consciousness, with its capacity for deeper perception and understanding, is not merely a feature of human life but an evolutionary endowment that characterizes all creation at the cosmic and planetary levels alike. Birth and death are not merely human experiences; they characterize the whole of God's creation. On the planetary scale earthquakes serve as a good example. Metaphorically, an earthquake can be described as the earth releasing its pent-up energies so that it can continue to grow and flourish in a more creative way. Without earthquakes, we would have no earth, nor would any of us be around even to speculate on this baffling paradox of birth-death-rebirth.

So, does God will the death of 240,000 innocent people, as happened in Pakistan in 2005, or of wholesale environmental catastrophe such as that resulting from the 2004 Asian tsunami? There is no logical or rational answer to this question because we are engaging a form of wisdom that is beyond rationality. Comparing the 2005 Pakistan quake with a stronger quake on the island of Guam in 1991 may help us reapproach the paradox. The quake in Pakistan registered at 7.4 on the Richter scale and led to 240,000 deaths. The 1991 Guam quake registered 8.0 and resulted in no human fatalities. As a colony of the United States, Guam's buildings were built with expensive attention to earthquake resistance. Pakistan, a significantly poorer country, could not afford to build such buildings. It quickly becomes obvious that the problem is not with the earthquake, or with God, but with the avaricious humans—the imperial Anthropocene—who choose not to share resources equally and justly across the human population.

Neither God nor the earthquake killed 240,000 people in Pakistan. Fellow humans caused the slaughter, addicted to the unjust distribution of earthly and human resources. We know how to cope with earthquakes, as the case of Guam in 1991 clearly shows. We could do so universally if we were committed to justice and equality all around. In terms of the recurring cycle of birth-death-rebirth (often described in Christian language as the paschal journey), here we encounter the daunting challenge: Can we patriarchal humans, addicted to domination and control, die to our power compulsion so that we can be raised to a more egalitarian, mutually empowering way of being for our own benefit and that of all creation? What is the point of clinging so tenaciously to the power-hungry Anthropocene?

Admittedly, we cannot always find a meaningful or reasonable explanation for those freaks of nature that wreak havoc on various lifeforms. When dealing with paradox, there will always be untidy elements that transcend rational explanation. Even in such situations we need to press the human dimension. In August 2005, Hurricane Katrina devastated the city of New Orleans; and Superstorm Sandy raged along the East Coast of the United States in October 2012. Nothing to do with humans, we are quick to retort! A capricious act of God, others suggest! In the wake of Katrina, commentators noted that hurricanes seem to come with a much greater ferocity than previously recorded. Other environmentally related factors, like global warming, may be contributing factors, which immediately raises suspicion of human contributions as we slowly and gradually realize that indirect human interference may well be a critical factor in several major natural catastrophes as it reinforces a range of ecological imbalances.

While we cannot be certain about the human role in natural catastrophes, it is becoming increasingly clear that human behavior contributes significantly to many forms of meaningless suffering on our earth. In recent times this has struck home with the devastating impact of the COVID-19 pandemic in 2020–22. Indeed, all the major pandemics of recent times—AIDS/HIV, MERS, SARS, and COVID-19—seem to have resulted from the spillover emanating from animals, birds, or mammals subjected to excessive human manipulation (see Quammen 2012). Did we bring these pandemics on ourselves? Are we ourselves largely responsible for many of the "evils" that befall us?

Only when we become aware of the great paradox will we gradually begin to realize that most of the meaningless suffering within and around us is actually caused by humans, not by God or by natural catastrophes. Our ignorance of the great paradox, and our inability (or unwillingness?) to engage it proactively is at the root of most, if not all, of the meaningless suffering in the world today.

The Meaning of Suffering

Suffering is not merely a human phenomenon. It affects all organic creatures and, most disturbing of all, spreads across a wide range of lifeforms. Suffering here denotes not merely personal pain and anguish, or merely the human inability to function fully in society, but rather the breakdown of the interdependence that enables and empowers flourishing for all sentient beings. In her personal blog of March 18, 2020, Vandana Shiva, physicist, social activist, and founder of the Research Foundation for Science, Technology, and Natural Resource Policy (RFSTN), writes:

> Over the past 50 years, up to 300 new pathogens have emerged. It is well documented that around 70 percent of the human pathogens, including HIV, Ebola, Influenza, MERS and SARS emerged when the forest ecosystems were invaded, and viruses jumped from animals to humans. When animals are cramped in factory farms, new diseases like swine flu and bird flu spring up and spread.

Flourishing entails pain and struggle, but not of the type extensively and brutally activated in the name of human power and progress.

Recognizing such a vital yet subtle distinction brings us to another central tenet of eco-spirituality: a universe without pain and suffering is simply impossible. Suffering in itself is endemic to every evolutionary breakthrough, desired by our creative God. Suffering is not the problem; our faulty perceptions cause the problem. We need to change, not the messy world that has been messed up in the first place by our reckless interference.

In the invitation to a whole new way of engagement with life, we need to acquaint ourselves with a critically important distinction between *paradox* and *flaw*. We frequently confuse these two features. Major religions, particularly Christianity and Islam, invoke the notion of a fundamental flaw to make rational sense of all the wrongs in our world.[2] When we do this, we seek out scapegoats to blame for all that is wrong, and invariably we end up trying to persecute or eliminate the scapegoat, tending to make the problems even more intractable.

As we enter more deeply into the world of paradox and learn to internalize its evolutionary meaning, it becomes progressively clear that there are no flaws anywhere in creation. What we call flaws are actually paradoxes in disguise. I am not suggesting we inhabit something akin to a perfect creation, because a paradoxical universe can never be perfect in any sense of the word. Invoking the notion of flaw, however, is a road to nowhere. It camouflages the rich meaning of paradox, undermines our integrity as paradoxical

---

[2] Christianity names it original sin, the history and nature of which I outline in a previous work (O'Murchu 2018).

creatures ourselves, and ultimately offers no meaningful resolution to our predicament of pain and suffering.

Because ours is a paradoxical creation, things will always be messy and untidy (not flawed), and it seems that for most of our time on earth we humans did not have a major problem with our paradoxical reality nor were we overwhelmed by the hardships and struggles that were part of our daily lot. Intuitively we knew the paradox upon which all creation evolves and flourishes. Rather than trying to rationalize such a contradiction (the scholarly expectation of our time) or get rid of such an anomaly (the solution proposed by both science and religion), our ancient ancestors learned to befriend the paradox, bringing their earth-focused wisdom and creativity to their engagement with it.

This quality of response is elegantly illustrated during the tsunami of December 2004. On the islands and coastal region of the Andaman Sea, on the west coast of Thailand, dwell a little-known Indigenous group, the Moken tribe. This Austronesian ethnic group, numbering no more than three thousand members, maintains a nomadic, sea-based culture. Scientists have discovered that their children can see like dolphins down to seventy-five feet under water, and that this improbable skill can be learned by any child.

As they gathered for breakfast on the morning of December 26, 2004, several members of the group noticed that the seawaters had receded to levels rarely seen, and fish were popping up and down like toy figures in a carnival game, striving to survive. Gathering for breakfast, they invoked the wisdom of the elders as they detected that nature was out of balance and wondered how they should respond.

The elders advised that, in a short time, those receded waters would return with a momentous and highly destructive force. The group took preemptive action, gathering as much as they could of their meager belongings and heading for higher ground where they knew they would be safe. On the way up, they met some Western tourists heading for the seafront. Unable to speak English, they urged the Westerners not to go down, but to little avail. As they went down, the tourists were trapped in the untimely waves and killed. A fortunate few scrambled their way back to higher ground and eventually reconnected with the Moken people. It was one of those lucky ones who told this story to the Western media.

Widely regarded as a primitive, ignorant group of people because they have little access to formal education, the Moken people are endowed with a wisdom that has survival value and gives them access to the natural world to a degree that most Westerners have lost entirely. Perhaps more significant was the simple but profound discernment they did on that precarious morning as they wrestled with what theologian John Caputo describes as having been "overtaken by the world" (Caputo 2015, 179). The "God" they knew to be right there in the living energy of creation itself spoke deeply in their hearts, empowering them to see beneath waves of fear and act with a wisdom that surely must challenge the most sublime knowledge any of us in the West claim to have.

The lesson is as simple as it is profound. In the crisp words of Karen Armstrong, "In nature we have a harmony in which violence and beauty, terror and serenity, mysteriously coexist, defying our own restricted categories" (Armstrong 2022, 72). When we encounter the great paradoxes of creation, we must learn to flow with them, not resist them. If we choose to battle with them, we lose. Befriend the paradox so that the paradox can befriend us, and be open to receiving that paradoxical wisdom from a range of different sources!

Eco-Spirituality and the Reality of Death

Across many religious traditions death is perceived as a limitation or, worse still, an evil to be eliminated. Even people who can accept and tolerate the notion of paradox as outlined above still pursue the notion that death is an enigma that somehow does not fit with what we expect a meaningful life to be. Some religions ultimately resolve this dilemma by promising immortality after this death-infested existence, whether by resurrection in the Christian tradition or by reincarnation in the great Eastern religions.

In the 1980s, feminist theologian Rosemary Radford Ruether addressed this issue of immortality in *Sexism and God-Talk*. She suggests that the preoccupation with immortality is an outgrowth of a Western and male concern with self-perpetuation as well as an abstraction from the real-life processes of growing, birthing, and dying. She highlights what she calls the ontological assumption that deems humans to be superior to nonhuman creatures, with a divine right to live forever. Immortality translates into a patriarchal projection in which humans, particularly males, seek to become Gods who can rule and dominate forever (Ruether 1983).

Ruether proposes that we opt for a theology that moves away from thinking so much about the ego's everlastingness and instead accepts our own finiteness, embracing death as part of a natural matrix of humans and nonhumans, who spring from the earth and eventually return to it in a nutritive regenerative cycle. We are invited to reenvision survival after death within the larger web of cosmic and planetary life:

> In effect, our existence ceases as individuated ego/organism, and dissolves back into the cosmic matrix of matter/energy from which new centers of individuation arise. It is this matrix rather than our individuated centers of being that is "everlasting," that subsists underneath the coming to be and passing away of individualized beings and even planetary worlds. . . . That great matrix that supports the energy-matter of our individuated beings is itself the ground of all personhood as well. The great collective personhood is the Holy being in which our achievements and failures are gathered up, assimilated into the fabric of being, and carried forward into new possibilities. (Ruether 1983, 257–58)

Rather than hoping for the ideal in the next life, she urges us to use this present moment to create "new possibilities" for a just and good communal existence for all sentient beings. Instead of the spirituality of seeking to escape this vale of tears to fulfillment in another world, let us commit to recreating life on earth as an enduring evolutionary paradise.

Paradoxically, religion is no longer the chief advocate for immortality. Modern science promotes immortality with a fervor rapidly outpacing religion, in a pursuit variously named by the naturalist Melanie Challenger as biological immortality or electronic immortality (Challenger 2021, 183).[3] A range of scientific gurus, including the futurist Ray

---

[3] Biological immortality is postulated on the basis of an enzyme called telomerase, which repairs those endings of DNA that shorten

Kurzweil (2005), are exploring ways in which artificial intelligence might confer a kind of digital immortality, preserving the personalities of the departed in virtual form in the hope that they will be able to further evolve in the future. In the desert climate of Scottsdale, Arizona, 147 brains and bodies rest, frozen in liquid nitrogen, with the goal of being revived one day. An estimated thirty-seven-thousand people have already signed up for a service known as Eternime, which plans to combine one's online footprint—made up of everything one has ever posted on social media, thoughts, smartphone pictures, and so on—with artificial intelligence to create a digital version of the person.[4]

Contrary to the religious and scientific pursuits of immortality, eco-spirituality unambiguously and unashamedly accepts and affirms death as an integral dimension of all lifeforms, from the vast galactic structures to the tiniest subatomic particles. Humans are not in any way exempt from such decay and disintegration. Death is an integral dimension of the great paradox through which evolution transpires and flourishes in every realm of creation.

Human exceptionalism to such an outcome is, in evolutionary terms, a relatively recent development, largely associated with the notion of a soul with which allegedly humans are uniquely endowed, bestowing an elevated and privileged ability to outlive all other mortal beings.

---

as we age. Electronic immortality is postulated on the fusion of the biological with electronic machinery, via pills like RTB101, seeking to reduce the aging of our immune systems. *Rejuvenate* or *Adcancells* are purported treatments that seek to alter the life potential of human stem cells.

[4] For a brief and an informed overview, see the You Tube presentation "Quantum Predicts Life after Death" from another reputable futurist, the popular physicist Michio Kaku. Further elaboration is in his book *The Future of Humanity* (Kaku 2018).

The primary evidence for such a phenomenon comes from classical Greek times, notably from the philosophers Socrates (d. 399 BCE), Plato (d. 348 BCE), and Aristotle (d. 322 BCE), all of whom understood that the soul had a kind of divine potency that enabled humans (especially men) to live according to the norms of reason and rationality.[5]

Because of its divine nature, the soul survives human death, and thereafter it is transformed into angelic status in the heavenly realm well away from this sinful world. Death, therefore, offers a double deliverance: first, from the fragility of our earthly condition; and second, from the curse of death itself. According to the Christian religion, this double deliverance was made possible by the death and rising to life again of the historical Jesus. Paradoxically, the curse of death gets even worse after the time of Jesus, and Christianity itself often resorted to the extermination and untimely deaths of those it considered to be its adversaries.

For eco-spirituality, restoring death to a more dignified status is a perennial challenge, one aptly and boldly reenvisioned by biologist Andreas Weber:

> The relationship between life and death is not simple or unambiguous. Stubbornly insisting on life can result in the opposite. The frantic desire to ward off death can actually invite it. Conversely, if you wish for life you must be prepared to welcome death. If you demand life, you must accept that death is a part of life, its dark half, without which no life, no experience, no living meaning, no poetry, and no love is possible. . . .

---

[5] We see a similar claim in the writings of St. Augustine, who claimed that for the human person, the soul was a special substance, endowed with reason, adapted to rule the body.

Wishing for life at any price continuously calls forth death—the death of other people, other beings, the extinguishing of languages, ideas, and, worst of all, possibilities and degrees of freedom. (Weber 2014, 60, 72)

Such an approach to death and dying requires some massive adjustments to how we currently understand our place in the scheme of things. It calls forth changes that shake the very foundations upon which our current civilization flourishes. These include:

1. All our educational systems need to highlight the paradoxical nature of life in our world and the wisdom needed to engage and befriend that paradox in our daily lives.
2. The biological portals of birth and death need to be seen as complementary forces propelling evolution of all life in its forward trajectory. Both experiences need our deepest respect and attention.
3. Religions need to confront the ideological cult of immortality and the resulting demonization of dying and death. Religious rituals, particularly those of Indigenous Peoples, can inform and enrich our engagement with death.
4. Anthropologically, we are likely to engage death more creatively and responsibly if we learn to live in accordance with the seasonal transformations of the natural world, where the complementarity of life and death is so transparent, although not always nice for the human to witness.
5. In the Christian narrative we need to revisit, reinterpret, and recast our soteriology, the elaborate claims

and interpretations of the Gospel that Jesus died for our sins and that his death (and resurrection) is the kernel of our salvation. We need to reenvision the death of Jesus as the prophetic price paid for a life radically lived for justice and empowerment. Salvation is in the commitment to life and not in the pursuit of death for its own sake (for more, see Johnson 2018; O'Murchu 2017).

6. Similarly, we must attend to the Christian narrative of the resurrection of Jesus. Employing the rhetoric of destroying death forever in order to enter the glory of an inflated divine imperialism is not healthy. I suggest that a more authentic discernment will lead us toward understanding the resurrection of Jesus as a rising up to new life and hope as evidenced through the first witnesses of the post-resurrection time.[6]

Eternal Life in the Midst of Creation

The present chapter seeks to challenge and counteract the ambivalence that various religious traditions hold in regard to creation and our place within it. Contrary to the widespread spirituality of escape, eco-spirituality invites us to consider the cosmic-earthly creation itself as the primary locus in which we encounter the living God, the energizing and animating Spirit who enlivens all that exists.

---

[6] In our standard biblical faith it is generally assumed that the first witnesses experiencing the empowerment of being raised up were the twelve male apostles. A closer reading of the resurrection narratives in all four Gospels do not support this interpretation. It is those described as "the women," with Mary Magdalene as their inspiring force, who are, in fact, the first witnesses (for more, see O'Murchu 2019).

That enlivening is mediated through the empowering energy of unconditional love. In our belonging to this creative enterprise, not in seeking to escape from it, we grow into that fuller sense of life and meaning that God and the universe desire for all. Yes, we are loved unconditionally and called to love all other beings unconditionally, and this can only be achieved in a creation imbued with freedom and creativity. That means that we inhabit a creation of high risk, which, in the present chapter, I have described as the great paradox of creation-cum-destruction. It is easy to love when everything is working to our human benefit, as we would like it to be. But for much of our life trajectory, it is not smooth sailing, and at times the challenges facing us can seem almost insurmountable. This is where true love—and above all, unconditional love—is put to the test.

Amid the light and the darkness, the promise and the peril, the breakthrough and the breakdown, the Great Spirit weaves the intricate web of life in the context of both cosmic and personal evolution. Andreas Weber invites us forward with these words:

> We are able to understand the nature of creative reality precisely because we, like all life-forms, are part of this reality. We are the world. We have both embodied and genuinely creative experiences with imagination, creativity, and freedom. We express our being in the world by the same means the world forms us. Reality is fluid and constantly bringing forth new beginnings— and so is our intercourse with it. (Weber 2014, 89)

Our journey is promising, exciting, and hope filled, but it is not without chaos, pain, and suffering inherent to the great paradox of universal life. As evolutionary theologian Ilia

Delio suggests, therein we will truly meet that foundational source we call God:

> We constantly pray to God to make order of our chaotic lives, but what if God is the very source of our chaos? What if chaos and disorder are not to be shunned and avoided but attended to and embraced? Nature shows us that life is not meant to be nice, neat and controlled but lived on the edge between order and disorder. Perhaps what we need is not planned retreats but unplanned contemplation that can take place anywhere and anytime—the alert mind in a dynamic world. (Delio 2021, 9)

Hopefully, the reflections of this book, and of the present chapter particularly, open new apertures for contemplating that paradoxical mystery, alerting our minds and our entire beings to the dynamic creation that nourishes and sustains meaning for every living being.

The mystics of several religious traditions describe this paradox as the dark night of the senses or the dark night of the soul. When it comes to eco-spirituality, however, we need to stretch that inherited human understanding to our engagement with the whole creation. The impending darkness invites a response of purification and illumination into the great paradoxical mystery that underpins all life—human and nonhuman alike.

Critical Issues for Ongoing Discernment

1. Any spirituality that tries to dodge the dark and painful side of reality is of little value to either humans or creation at large. It fails to engage the paradox at the heart of creation, holding both creativity and destruction as God-given dimensions of our evolving universe.

2. This paradox (of creation-cum-destruction) has nothing to do with a fundamental flaw. There is no flaw in God's creation, but there is an enormous amount of paradox, and the major religions badly confuse the two elements.

3. While mainline religions seek to get rid of pain, suffering, and death, eco-spirituality embraces all these elements and seeks their transformation through a process of befriending the paradox rather than seeking to eliminate the dark side of life.

4. Most of the meaningless suffering within and around us *is actually caused by humans*, not by God or by natural catastrophes. Our ignorance of the great paradox and our inability (or unwillingness?) to engage it are at the root of most if not all the meaningless suffering in the world today.

5. Because of their closeness to the natural world, the ancients, somewhat like contemporary Indigenous Peoples, knew a convivial relationship with the living universe, experiencing the daily interaction of life and death, creation and destruction, without—it

seems—our contemporary compulsion for domination and control.

6. Contrary to the religions, on the one hand, and the scientific pursuit of immortality, on the other, eco-spirituality unambiguously and unashamedly accepts and affirms death as an integral dimension of all life-forms, from the vast galactic structures to the tiniest subatomic particles.

7. "Nature shows us that life is not meant to be nice, neat, and controlled but lived on the edge between order and disorder. Perhaps what we need is not planned retreats but unplanned contemplation that can take place anywhere and anytime—the alert mind in a dynamic world" (Delio 2021, 9).

7

Nature's Secrets Can Re-create the World

We are beginning to recover a sense that the simple act of gazing, of paying attention—one of the most ancient and enduring ways of understanding contemplative practice—can open up a space in the soul, a space in which the world may live and move in us. And that we are being called to renew our commitment to this work—for the sake of the world.

—Douglas E. Christie

To glimpse the sacrality of the natural world requires a degree of quiet and solitude that is hard to come by today.

—Karen Armstrong

Eco-spirituality is unashamedly secular, earthly, and materialistic "for the sake of the world," marking a radical departure from the former spirituality of seeking escape from this world. Eco-spirituality is very much at home in the ordinary and forever open to being surprised by the extraordinary-in-the-ordinary, peering out at us through the lattice of dirt, soil, air, and water. It "feels" meaning in

115

every life encounter. In fact, *feeling* is the primary medium through which it connects with the sacred and encounters its mysterious animation.

As we begin to feel our way in and through the natural world, we begin to transcend the rational, functional consciousness of viewing life as an amalgam of objects put there for our sole use and benefit. We feel our way into a range of connectivity. For biologist Andreas Weber, "the new biology considers the phenomenon of feeling as the primary explanation, not only of consciousness, but of all life processes" (Weber 2016, 4). Elaborating further, Weber writes, "Feeling is much more basic and existential. It is an experience and a formative power that binds an organism together. Matter is not able to be real without feeling. . . . Feeling without matter is impossible. What we experience inwardly as emotion is something that happens outwardly to ourselves as bodies" (Weber 2016, 96, 109).

Nature feels different, and we perceive ever new ways of engaging with the reality of our world. This opens up new vistas for us to become ethical, ecological beings. Eco-spirituality is deeply ethical in calling forth new ways to connect with life at large, particularly within the context of our daily encounters with the natural world.

Ever Heard of Biomimicry?

As inwardness is the necessary way bodies experience themselves, feeling is also a crucial component of an ecological ethics. To be connected is always an existential engagement, and this echoes as feeling. Feeling is, so to speak, the core self of a commons ethic. It symbolizes how well the mutual realization of individuality and the whole are achieved (Weber 2016, 355ff.).

Such emotional connectedness has nothing to do with myopic narcissistic sentimentality—an accusation often leveled against people claiming to be spiritual but not religious—but becomes a perceptual wisdom that begins to see what systems theorist Jeremy Lent calls the "patterning instinct" across several life structures (Lent 2017).[1] It can evolve into what visionaries like Douglas E. Christie describe as a contemplative gaze (Christie 2013). Christie, along with many others, has been inspired by the prescient observations of Thomas Merton, who already in 1961 had written:

> Contemplation is the highest expression of our intellectual and spiritual life. It is that life itself, fully awake, fully active. It is spiritual wonder. It is spontaneous awe at the wonder of life, of being. It is gratitude for life, for awareness, for being. It is a vivid realization of the fact that life and being in us proceed from an invisible, transcendent and infinitely abundant Source. (Merton 1961, 1)

If we can remain long enough, feeling our way with and through this enduring intensity of presence, I do not think we can escape the organic empowering mystery staring us in the face at every one of life's turns. With the perception and immersion of naturalists like Weber and Christie, we can attend to the inner essence, the womb of our becoming, the nurturing breast that provides our daily food, and the creative vitality that awakens our imaginations,

---

[1] Science writer Brian Clegg is one of the notable endorsers of Lent's observations (see Clegg 2021).

intuitions, and sense of mystery. Another naturalist, David Abram, writes:

> In a thoroughly palpable sense, we are born of this planet, our attentive bodies co-evolved in rich and intimate rapport with the other bodily forms—animals, plants, mountains, rivers—that compose the shifting flesh of this breathing world. . . . Sensory perception is the silken web that binds our separate nervous systems into the encompassing ecosystem. (Abram 2010, 78, 134)

When we become more acquainted with the natural world and, more important, when we begin to internalize its creative dynamics, we progressively begin to realize that nature's wisdom also provides the ideal prototypes for how we should engage with nature. One emerging expression of this natural wisdom is known as *biomimicry*, which describes how we can imitate the models, systems, and elements of nature for the purpose of solving complex human problems.[2] Biomimicry examines the extraordinary innovations of the natural world and the human inventions they have inspired.

---

[2] The term *biomimicry* appeared as early as 1982 and was popularized by scientist and author Janine Benyus in her 1997 book *Biomimicry: Innovation Inspired by Nature,* where *biomimicry* is defined as a new science that studies nature's models and then imitates or takes inspiration from these designs and processes to solve human problems. Benyus suggests that we look at nature as a "Model, Measure, and Mentor" and emphasizes sustainability as an objective of biomimicry (Benyus 1997). For a simple illustrated introduction, see Dora Lee (2011) or Jennifer Swanson (2020); for a more elaborate updated overview, with several practical examples, see Dayna Baumeister (2014).

Biomimicry is an approach to innovation that seeks sustainable solutions to human challenges by emulating nature's time-tested patterns and strategies. The core idea is that nature has already solved many of the problems with which we are grappling. The goal is to create products, processes, and policies—new ways of living—that are well adapted to life on earth over the long haul; to this end, animals, plants, and microbes are the consummate engineers. Biomimicry is now the subject of intensive research and study. The following examples give a tangible sense of what is involved, opening implications for eco-spirituality.

1. The *kingfisher* is a small, brightly colored bird with a unique streamlined beak. It is found on all continents apart from Antarctica. Throughout Japan the sleek front ends of bullet trains are based on the long, streamlined beak of the kingfisher, enabling faster speeds while also resolving unacceptable noise pollution.

2. *Geckos* are small, mostly carnivorous lizards found in warm climates throughout the world. They range in size from approximately half an inch to twenty-four inches. Regardless of their size, all geckos have the ability to stick to practically anything, not because they have some unique kind of glue on their toes, but because they have millions of tiny, nano-size hairs.[3] These microscopic hairs grip objects extremely well, inspiring a range of biometric creations such as medical bandages coated with a special type of glue that contains thousands of microscopic grippers that

---

[3] Worth remembering here is that a single strand of human hair can range between 60,000 and 100,000 nanometers.

stick to the skin and wall-climbing pads designed from nano-size fibers. NASA is currently exploring this nanotechnology in order to attach sensors to satellites both inside and outside the station. What a service to humankind from this fascinating creature!

3. Marine aquariums may display colorful, mushroom-shaped corals. They are called *discosoma*. One particular type, with red fluorescent color, is known to be rich in proteins. It is now being used by a biotechnology company called Werewool to design fibers for sustainable textiles, with inherent properties such as color, moisture management, and stretch that meet the demands of today's consumers. Such textiles are created without the need for toxic dyes, finishes, and petroleum-based synthetics.

4. A *beetle* found mainly in the sand dunes of Africa's Namib Desert survives in such very dry conditions thanks to bumps on its back that can collect water from morning fog. The water particles cling to the bumps and accumulate to the point where they run off the beetle's back and into its mouth. Scientists are exploring how to use this facility to provide much-needed water to various drought situations around the world at a quicker and cheaper rate than using conventional pipes and tanks (Swanson 2020, 60–61).

5. The slime—a mucus—left behind by a *garden slug* is essential; without this crystal-containing goo, the slug couldn't move. Alternatively, when it feels the threat of attack (for example, from a bird), the slug excretes a stronger type of glue with which it can cling rigidly to an object. Scientists have been

exploring a range of adhesive tapes for medical and technological use based on this rich natural resource.

6. Prosthetic limbs have often been inspired by nonhuman creatures, for example, octopuses and cheetahs. Two-thirds of an *octopus's* neurons and brain cells are found in its eight bendable arms. They are currently being explored for their potential to create new forms of prosthetic limbs, particularly arms. The first running blade—the Flex-Foot—was designed by Van Phillips in the 1970s. Phillips was an American inventor and an amputee himself. He studied ligaments that store muscle energy, observing the tendons of porpoises, kangaroos and cheetahs, noting how the *cheetah's* hind leg lands and compresses within its innate elasticity. In fact, one of the leading world companies for producing such running blades, the Icelandic Össur, has named several of its blades after the cheetah.

7. In 2011, Yale students made headlines with the discovery of a mushroom fungus in Ecuador, *Pestalotiopsis microspora,* that has the ability to digest and break down polyurethane plastic, even in an oxygen-free (anaerobic) environment, which might make it effective at the bottom of landfills. Other researchers have continued to study the subject. In 2017, scientist Sehroon Khan and his research team at the World Agroforestry Centre in Kunming, China, discovered another biodegrading fungus in a landfill in Islamabad, Pakistan: *Aspergillus tubingensis.* This fungus is capable of colonizing polyester polyurethane (PU) and breaking it down it into smaller pieces within the span of two months.

8. The *sandcastle worm*, a mere three inches long, spends much of its life building honeycomb-shaped sand structures on rocky beaches, bonded firmly by a glue-like substance from the worm's own body. This substance does not dissolve in water. Scientists are exploring possible uses for this glue to repair human limbs and even repair broken teeth.

9. A bulky insect known as the *clanger cicada* uses its wings to kill bacteria on contact. Inspired by this biometric natural resource, scientists are working to create a substance that can be used in public places to get rid of undesirable bacteria.

10. Having studied the collaborative endeavor of *bee colonies*, Regen Energy created a new electrical grid into a communication network capable of maximizing efficiency in order to balance loads during peak-power periods.

As illustrated in the growing literature on this exciting and empowering discovery of nature's deep wisdom, examples of biomimicry abound (Baumeister 2014; Harman 2014). We are witnessing a paradigm shift on an earth-body imbued with a wisdom many degrees more complex and empowering than human wisdom, reminding humans that there are more creative and dynamic ways to engage with life, strategies that are also far less violent and destructive than the ones we currently employ. Andreas Weber seeks to reclaim what he calls an "erotic ecology" endowed with a gifted generosity almost overwhelming in its graciousness:

In the natural world everything is gifted. From the sun's warmth to the sustenance that it donates to us, from the possibilities of deep self-understanding to the joy that results from it, nature's gifts are exuded as unconditional offerings. It is characteristic of the natural world to be life. We receive everything living free of charge. The vivacity that we experience in the old, densely interwoven network of relationship is an offering without expectation of return: an expression of life that enlivens. . . . If giving is a central ecological dimension, actually the center of any ecology, it follows that we must make it also into a cornerstone of a culture of life. (Weber 2014, 182–83)

Biomimicry is not merely a new revolutionary way of modeling life and technology on the principles of nature itself. It signifies a great deal more, a vivid reminder to us that all nature is about giftedness, a profound reciprocity that gives eco-spirituality an even more gracious meaning.

Ecological Engineering

Much of the wisdom gathered from this research is employed by contemporary engineers seeking to work collaboratively with nature and with the natural processes that sustain and promote life in a range of different ways. Ecological engineering may be described as the design of sustainable ecosystems that integrate human society with its natural environment for the benefit of both. Its goals include the restoration of ecosystems that have been substantially disturbed by human activities and the development of new sustainable ecosystems that have both human and ecological values.

Ecological engineering may be based on one or more of the following three classes of eco-technology:

1. Ecosystems are imitated or copied to reduce or solve a pollution problem, leading to constructed ecosystems. Fishponds and constructed wetlands for treating wastewater or diffuse pollution sources are examples.

2. Ecosystems are recovered after significant disturbances. Coal-mine reclamation and restoration of lakes and rivers are examples.

3. Ecosystems are used for the benefit of humanity without destroying the ecological balance, that is, the utilization of ecosystems on an ecologically sound basis. Typical examples are the use of integrated agriculture and development of organic agriculture. This type of eco-technology finds wide application in the ecological management of renewable resources.[4]

The balance between human desire and the actual well-being of the ecosystem is a major challenge facing ecological engineering. Eco-spirituality seems essential to the wisdom needed for the desired integration of the human and the natural world, faced as we are with enormous contemporary challenges such as global warming and the need to reduce our use of fossil fuels.

A deeper appreciation of nature's own wisdom, as exemplified in biomimicry, certainly helps to change and move

---

[4] These three classes were developed by Sven Erik Jorgensen. The research of William J. Mitsch and Sven Erik Jorgensen (2004), highlighting five basic concepts that differentiate the ecological from other approaches in ways that benefit society and nature, is worthy of note: (1) it is based on the self-designing capacity of ecosystems; (2) it can be the field (or acid) test of ecological theories; (3) it relies on system approaches; (4) it conserves nonrenewable energy sources; and (5) it supports ecosystem and biological conservation.

our human consciousness in the direction of this desired integration. It will also be one of the more effective means for alleviating the eco-anxiety of our time. The social, economic, and political consequences are formidable, and we hope that things do not have to get considerably worse before the human species awakens to the urgency of this time. Such awakening is a primary goal of contemporary eco-spirituality.

Technology Supporting Eco-Spirituality

The noble and exciting possibilities of developments like biomimicry and ecological engineering need to be considered within the controversial realm of modern technology, with its promise and peril. There is no doubt that computing and digital technology have changed the institutions of society and that the rate of change is accelerating. We have seen its benefits in healthcare, education, trans-global communication, and in virtually every sphere of contemporary life, including the transmission of religion and its ideals.

In her 2009 book *Technology and Religion* theologian and computer scientist Noreen Herzfeld approaches the field from three different angles: technologies of the human body—such as genetic engineering, stem cells, cloning, pharmaceutical technologies, mechanical enhancement and cyborgs; technologies of the human mind—like human and artificial intelligence, virtual reality and cyberspace; and technologies of the external environment—such as nanotechnology, genetically modified crops and new agricultural technologies, and energy technology. Like several commentators of the past fifty years, she outlines the benefits of each while raising several questions for the monotheistic religions on how such advances distract from, and can even undermine, inherited faith and morality.

Our lives have now become so technology oriented that it is almost impossible to spend a day without a gadget in our hands. A "new normal" has caught us almost unawares: an iPhone in one's pocket, an iPad in one's purse, and a laptop in one's bag all syncing every fifteen minutes with Facebook, Twitter, and whatever one calls an office. Websites and other apps are designed to scour other Facebook pages, websites, newsfeeds, and blogs on our behalf, signaling every time a topic of personal interest appears. Eyes look down to laps instead of up to a teacher, checking a handheld screen for whatever's being "pushed" toward us.

Even in social company people often slide into a kind of connected isolationism, in which ordinary conversational connection seems to be undermined by the near-addictive grip within which the machine holds us. We tend to exalt the value of such connectedness without acknowledging the serrating effect it can have on our senses, our emotions, our relationships, and our need for times of solitude and quiet. From a spiritual perspective the electronic gadgetry can easily become a compensatory "god" on whom we depend for the satisfaction and fulfillment of our most basic needs.

Beyond the impact on the human psyche, extensive automation of the human body is emerging, ranging from the widespread demand for cosmetic surgery to cyborg alignments employed today to modify and assist several of our bodily functions. Indisputably, many of these developments have enhanced the quality of human health and well-being, leaving us, however, with a confused and uncertain moral landscape. Instead of relying on the healing endowments of nature, are we unreflectively handing over our healthcare to ever more mechanistic resolutions, while neglecting, and even undermining, the resourcefulness of our natural (God-given) human immunity? As we increase the external reliance on such medical interventions, are we inadvertently neglecting our interior resilience, with its innate potential for spiritual well-being?

Finally, we also need to attend to what Polish sociologist Zygmunt Bauman calls "liquid capitalism,"[5] focused on electronic, mediated, and short-term outcomes, with high production design and always catchy labels. Increasingly, everything in creation is viewed as an object, a commodity to be bartered and discarded when no longer useful to feed voracious human consumption. At this level ecological devastation becomes an ever-increasing problem for our contemporary world.

If we could look back into deep time, we would probably note that new technologies were always received with apprehension and fear. Only with hindsight are we able to see that, in most cases, the benefits outweighed the disadvantages and evolutionary progress only becomes apparent long after the initial confusing breakthrough. We can, therefore, consider contemporary technological developments—like the rapid emergence of artificial intelligence (AI)—to carry a positive and empowering potential, provided their emergence is safeguarded with that quality of integration posited by astronomer Carl Sagan:

Many of the dangers we face arise indeed from science and technology—but, more fundamentally, because we have become powerful without becoming

---

[5] Bauman first coined the term *liquid capitalism* in the early years of the present century to describe the unpredictability and unreliability of current market practices, reinforcing ever greater levels of insecurity in society generally (for more, see Bauman 2000).

commensurately wise. The world-altering powers that technology has delivered into our hands now require a degree of consideration and foresight that has never before been asked of us. (Sagan 1994, 316)

Tomas Chamorro-Premuzic is one of the many scholars tackling the urgent question of AI and its impact on the human species. (Chamorro-Premuzic 2023). AI is changing the ways we live, work, love, and entertain ourselves. Dating apps are using AI to pick our potential partners. Retailers are using AI to predict our behavior and desires. Rogue actors are bombarding us with misinformation on a daily basis. Companies are using AI to hire us—or not. Though AI has the potential to change our lives for the better, it is also worsening our bad tendencies, making us more distracted, selfish, biased, narcissistic, unpredictable, and impatient. We can't get rid of it. So, how do we wrestle with it so that we benefit from its positive potential rather than be destroyed by its manipulative force?

These, then, are some of the initiatives the human species needs to embrace if the emerging technological revolution is to be one of promise and hope for both humanity and the earth we inhabit.

1. Our educational systems—at all levels—need to transcend the current fixation on power and progress, and instead opt for critical discerning skills to differentiate good outcomes from potentially destructive ones.

2. Whenever possible, we need to realign our technologies with the inherited wisdom of the natural world (as in biomimicry), thus employing technology to

support organic evolution rather than undermine or destroy it.

3. In this geological epoch of the Anthropocene, we need to outgrow the imperial destructive domination that has characterized our species over recent millennia and come to terms with the fact that we are a servant species that can only hope to survive—and evolve—by developing radical new ways to engage collaboratively with other lifeforms.

4. We need to outgrow the highly destructive dualistic splitting of the sacred and the secular so that our economics, politics, and social policies can incorporate spiritual values into all our engagements with the web of life.

5. We need to extend our various notions of morality beyond the human realm to include all our interactions with the wider spheres of planetary life. Perhaps this should be the prerogative of an international body like the United Nations.

6. Our elected parliamentarians and their advisers need to be selected not on the basis of inherited party politics, based on outdated patriarchal power and domination, but on the ability to dialogue intelligibly on the major ethical and moral issues confronting us today, particularly in the technological sphere.

7. Ronald J. Brown (2018), coming from a Unitarian perspective, suggests that the major world religions will need to undergo extensive reform if they are to stand any chance of informing and influencing our emerging technological world. In my opinion, the eco-spiritual vision of the present work stands a better chance at engaging the complex evolutionary issues confronting humanity today.

Eco-Spirituality, Technology, and Morality

By the mid-twenty-first century, medical technology will have developed a range of brain implants that will be capable of changing several features of human behavior. And such technology will be available to anybody wishing to make such changes simply by visiting a local doctor's surgery. Such advances are popularly hailed as a positive breakthrough for the well-being and progress of humanity, projecting our species into the new realm of the so-called posthuman.

Developments of this nature raise a range of ethical questions in a current cultural landscape within which ethics and morality are often compromised in the name of money, power, and progress. For Toby Ord and other recent analysts, this leaves us in a precarious space of *existential risk* that threatens the destruction of humanity's long-term potential (Ord 2020, 37).[6] I find the use of this term too narrowly confined to the precarious future of the human species, an existential vulnerability entwined with humanity's often brutal treatment of the other lifeforms that share Planet Earth with us. For eco-spirituality, the existential threats to humanity should never be viewed in isolation nor should

---

[6] This notion of existential risk (with a particular concern for the future of humanity) was first outlined by the British/Canadian philosopher John A. Leslie in his 1996 book *The End of the World*. The notion was further refined and popularized by the Swedish, Oxford-based philosopher Nick Bostrom, who, in 2005, founded the Future of Humanity Institute, which researches the far future of human civilization. He is also an adviser to the Centre for the Study of Existential Risk. Much of Bostrom's extensive analysis and research is synthesized by Ord in his popular book *The Precipice* (Ord 2020).

they be prized more highly than those experienced by all other sentient beings.

The most serious ethical dilemmas facing humanity today are no longer those that pertain merely to human values and behavior. The moral dilemmas related to the treatment of other species, of earth's resources, and in relevant major issues such as climate change are far more complex and of greater moral urgency. In the collapse of religion as a leading cultural and moral force, ethical deprivation has emerged as a major dilemma facing the human species. Until the mid twentieth century, religious traditions provided the vanguard for ethical standards and moral guidelines, particularly in the West. In several countries governments looked to churches and other religious groups to provide the moral barometer for responsible human action, personally and culturally. Even in those countries that enshrined a distinction between church and state in their constitutions, the moral prerogative of the major religions remained an important resource for ethical governance.

Such reliance on religion has largely evaporated in the Western world, and that creates even further resistance to religious influence in several other contemporary situations. Religion, for the greater part, is no longer capable of delivering a relevant ethics for the complex issues facing humanity in the twenty-first century. From here on, we will have to rely on governments to provide the moral guidelines, an undertaking for which most parliamentarians feel largely unprepared and a mandate that feels overwhelming for several government institutions.

Momentous and complex though these issues are, an eco-spirituality of our time needs to take them on board. Across all contemporary religions, spirituality tends to be regarded

as a personal or interpersonal matter, related to human holiness and personal well-being. Eco-spirituality must move
beyond the solely personal context, embracing the sacred
within all spheres of life, particularly in the context of the
major ecological challenges facing us today. That cannot be
done without engaging a range of ethical and moral issues
pertaining to life at large, and not merely to human behavior.

This enlarged ethical horizon is a wakeup call for all
human institutions in the twenty-first century, secular
and religious alike. The Earth Charter, at the end of the
twentieth century, prefigured *Laudato Si'* and can serve as
a crucial document for human societies around the planet
as we move forward.[7] By taking the Earth Charter as the
basis for morality and ethics in our time, we are formu-
lating an ethical code that is multidisciplinary in nature,
transcending our narrow anthropocentrism and extending
the spiritual significance of morality in the direction of a
deeper integration that mainline religions seem unable to
achieve on their own. To propel contemporary humans and
their institutions in that more liberating and empowering
direction, it seems to me that we need the more holistic
kind of spirituality outlined in the present work. Without
such an eco-spiritual imperative, the necessary motivation
and inspiration for such an undertaking will be lacking.

---

[7] The edited volume *The Crisis of Global Ethics and the Future
of Global Governance* (Burdon et al. 2019) is an admirable attempt
at exploring and integrating such a morality. In this book, leading figures in environmental ethics, philosophy, and law approach
questions surrounding global ethics and governance from a range
of cultural and philosophical perspectives. They base their reflections and recommendations on the principles outlined in the Earth
Charter drawn up between 1992 and 2002 to highlight the moral
dilemmas of our time and the ethical imperatives desired to address
these dilemmas.

What precisely would be involved in such an ethical horizon? What would be the key ingredients? What targets for implementation would be envisaged? The Millennium Project lists "15 Global Challenges." The 2023 list follows:

1. How can sustainable development be achieved for all while addressing global climate change?
2. How can everyone have sufficient clean water without conflict?
3. How can population growth and resources be brought into balance?
4. How can genuine democracy emerge from authoritarian regimes?
5. How can decision making be enhanced by integrating improved global foresight during unprecedented accelerating change?
6. How can the global convergence of information and communications technologies work for everyone?
7. How can ethical market economies be encouraged to help reduce the gap between rich and poor?
8. How can the threat of new and reemerging diseases and immune micro-organisms be reduced?
9. How can education make humanity more intelligent, knowledgeable, and wise enough to address its global challenges?
10. How can shared values and new security strategies reduce ethnic conflicts, terrorism, and the use of weapons of mass destruction?
11. How can the changing status of women help improve the human condition?
12. How can transnational organized crime networks be stopped from becoming more powerful and sophisticated global enterprises?

13. How can growing energy demands be met safely and efficiently?
14. How can scientific and technological breakthroughs be accelerated to improve the human condition?
15. How can ethical considerations become more routinely incorporated into global decisions?[8]

Though there is no reference to Church or religion, Christians would recognize every aspiration of the Sermon on the Mount in this list. The list also prefigures the radical earth-centered empowerment envisaged in the new reign of God (the new companionship). It supports and endorses the socioeconomic critique of recent Catholic popes Benedict XVI (2009) and Francis (2015; 2020), as well as The Canterbury Statement, *Stewards of Creation: A Hope-Filled Ecology*, jointly published by the Anglican Communion and the Orthodox Churches in October 2020.[9]

These goals for a better world are transnational in nature and trans-institutional in solution. They cannot be addressed by any government or institution acting alone. They require collaborative action among governments, religions, international organizations, corporations, universities, NGOs, and creative individuals. They transcend the dualistic splitting that has so damaged the entire web of life over several centuries, and they augur the brightest horizon of hope for humans and for all sentient beings on Planet Earth, now and for the long-term future.

---

[8] The list is updated yearly. For the most up-to-date list, see the millennium-project.org website.

[9] Other world religions have made significant contributions as well, as documented by Mary Evelyn Tucker and John Grim from the Center for the Study of World Religions at Harvard Divinity School (Tucker, Grim, and Jenkins 2017).

Universal Giftedness

Down through the centuries, poets and philosophers have hailed the glory of God radiant in creation; at a deeper level mystics have long celebrated the incarnational, embodied wisdom of creation itself. Eco-spirituality seeks to build on these foundations while also pursuing new levels of integration incorporating the diverse elements of our daily behaviors within the complex technological, social, economic, and political horizons of our time.

To protect the universal giftedness of creation, eco-spirituality aspires toward a new quality of integration, incorporating people and planet alike, seeking to rediscover a relevant and liberating ethics for our age, and immersing ourselves ever more deeply in the inherited contemplative traditions of our rich past. Supported by such a rich integration, we can witness more fully and directly the "in-spirited" (inspired) earth, manifesting in creatively elegant ways the divine will for life as a foundational organicity that is insinuated into every embodied lifeform.

Growing into contemplative practices of eco-spirituality, we grow into a deeper appropriation of our incarnational faith. As we relate anew to the presence of the Holy One in every impulse of creation, we recognize that faith does not emerge through evangelical fervor or notional assent to doctrinal propositions. Beyond even fidelity to a formal religious institution, eco-spirituality calls forth an enfleshed faith that gifts life throughout creation.

Critical Issues for Ongoing Discernment

1. When we become more acquainted with the natural world and begin to internalize its creative dynamics, we begin to realize that nature's wisdom also provides the ideal prototypes for how we should engage with the natural world. One emerging expression of this natural wisdom is *biomimicry,* which describes how we can imitate the models, systems, and elements of nature for the purpose of solving complex *human* problems.

2. As we begin to create products, processes, and policies—new ways of living—that are well adapted to life on earth, we come to understand that the animals, plants, and microbes are the consummate engineers, adopting strategies that are far less violent and destructive than the ones we currently employ.

3. Our lives have now become tech oriented. From a spiritual perspective our electronic gadgetry can easily become a compensatory "god" on which we depend for the satisfaction and fulfillment of our most basic needs.

4. For the greater part, technology seems to be an evolutionary development desired by our God, leaving humans with an enormous challenge to develop moral values and guidelines for the responsible use of such technology. For eco-spirituality, the Earth Charter provides a timely example highlighting our

current moral dilemmas and the ethical imperatives
desired to address these dilemmas.

5. As we engage the technological advances of our time,
   our educational systems—at all levels—need to transcend the current fixation on power and progress, and
   instead opt for critical discerning skills to differentiate
   good outcomes from potentially destructive ones.

6. Eco-spirituality is deeply ethical in calling forth new
   ways to connect with life at large, and particularly
   within the context our daily encounters with the natural world.

8

Eco-Spirituality and the Conscious Universe

Consciousness is at the core of an emerging spirituality in this quantum universe, for consciousness, like energy, is mysteriously pervasive. We speak of divine consciousness, yet all consciousness is divine. It is a mode of divinity whereby Spirit is present in and to and through each and every one of us and every aspect of creation.

—Miriam Therese Winter

There is every reason to hope that the new science of consciousness will lead to a new covenant with nature.

—Philip Goff

While the prefix *eco* immediately denotes an ecological dimension that now needs to be included in and aligned to our understanding of spirituality, it invites us into a vastly larger horizon of cosmic and global significance. The exploration of *consciousness* is central to this bigger picture. The scientific study of consciousness was all the rage in the late 1800s, largely inspired by William James's 1890 work *The Principles of Psychology*. Additionally, Jungian psychology delves deeply into the meaning of consciousness and makes the notion more accessible to the general public (see Edinger 1984). However, it was only toward the latter part of the twentieth century, with the advent of high-tech brain scanners, that consciousness became more acceptable in scientific discourse.

American philosopher and cognitive scientist Daniel Dennett, and his landmark book *Consciousness Explained* (1991), is a central figure in this discourse. For Dennett, consciousness is essentially a mechanistic process happening within the human brain, neurons interacting in response to various behavioral stimulations. It is a human phenomenon related to thought and perception, governed by brain activity.

Long associated with basic awareness and related psychological states of perception, feeling, intuition, and imagination, science is now stretching its meaning beyond the personal and interpersonal contexts into the very essence of creation itself. We not only need to include it in our search for a contemporary eco-spirituality, but it may well be a central feature, requiring a much deeper discerning analysis.

The Enlarged Horizon

The other and much more controversial dimension of consciousness studies is known as *panpsychism*, which claims that consciousness is inherent to even the tiniest pieces of matter—an idea that suggests the fundamental building blocks of reality have conscious experience. Some scientists, like Italian physicist Guido Tonelli, invoke the notion of the void—or creative vacuum—as foundational to the consciousness that permeates all creation. Tonelli writes:

> There is no more strictly ordered, regulated and symmetrical system than the void. Everything belonging to it is strictly codified, every particle of matter goes hand in hand with its corresponding antiparticle, every fluctuation dutifully observes the constraints of the uncertainty principle, everything moves to a cadenced and well-tempered rhythm, a perfect choreography without improvisation or virtuosic excess. (Tonelli 2021, 43)

The void of open space is anything but empty. It is a seething, breathing, pulsating force, fueled by a wisdom that defies rational explanation. Crucially, it implies consciousness that informs the entire universe. In the words of contemporary physicist Jude Currivan, "Consciousness isn't something we have; it's what we and the whole world are" (2017, 233).

This enlarged horizon has a particular appeal to scientists influenced by the vision of quantum physics. Paul Levy writes:

> Being fundamental, consciousness can't be reduced to other features of the universe such as energy or matter. Thinking that the source of consciousness is in the brain is like looking in the radio for the announcer. . . . The brain does not produce consciousness; it is an instrument that tunes into and transmits it. Rather than generating consciousness, the brain may simply be a transducer that acts as a filter as it mediates consciousness at the physical level. (Levy 2018, 279)

Ilia Delio adds: "Consciousness is not a human phenomenon; nor does it pertain to the human brain alone. . . . We have come to understand consciousness as a cosmic phenomenon.

Consciousness is integral to all aspects of cosmic life" (Delio 2015, 56, 58). In his detailed exploration of the patterning instinct across all aspects of universal life, systems theorist Jeremy Lent contends, "Consciousness is not something that happens to us; it's an ongoing activity emerging through our engagement with the world" (Lent 2021, 184).

Throughout this book I highlight a major challenge to our contemporary anthropology whereby we need to outgrow our species domination in favor of viewing ourselves as a derived species, one that depends on the life of the larger web for everything that constitutes our being and becoming. We exist, grow, and flourish because the creation we inhabit makes all that possible. And yet we are, like all other life organisms, totally unique. Our uniqueness, however, is not in lording it over all other lifeforms—as often understood by the mastery of life referenced in Genesis 1:26—but in bringing our uniqueness to the table of mutual interaction with all other living organisms. That uniqueness is often stated as follows: *We are creation becoming conscious of itself.*

Our self-consciousness and the consciousness of creation are of one and the same substance.[1] Having received from creation the capacity to be aware, the quality and depth of our awareness contributes to and enriches the consciousness of creation. The mutual enrichment of that process very much depends on the quality of our *attention* and *intention*. How sensitively aware are we to what is happening within and around us? What is the quality of intention (desiring) that we bring to all our life engagements?

---

[1] This can be understood as one fertile example of the *oneness* referenced in many of the great mystical traditions of our world (Fox 2011; Lent 2021).

Popular American counselor and psychotherapist Wayne Dyer describes human intentionality as a cosmic force inviting and challenging our human desiring. "Intention is not something you do, but rather a force that exists in the universe as an invisible field of energy. . . . Intention itself is a unified energy field that intends everything into existence" (Dyer 2004, 12, 135). Consequently, meaning arises from within, rather than being propelled by forces from outside. This is another foundational tenet to a view of the world arising from quantum physics and long known to the mystical traditions of our world.

Intelligence: Human and Artificial

Even if we cherish the notion of inhabiting a universe where consciousness is fundamentally benign and empowering—a view not espoused by the vast majority of humans—we cannot bypass movements of our time that foreground the desire for human control. We have already encountered this drive toward human supremacy in the technological advances of recent centuries. We also need to acknowledge how research into artificial general intelligence (AGI) is moving apace, with prospects for our human future that are both promising and perilous.[2]

Artificial intelligence (AI) was first developed in the 1950s in reference to the simulation of human intelligence in machines programmed to think like humans and mimic their actions. The term may also be applied to any machine that exhibits traits associated with a human mind, such as learning and problem solving. Many of us have seen robots

---

[2] Artificial general intelligence (AGI) is deemed to be more expansive than the earlier AI (artificial intelligence).

carry out a range of human tasks in an efficient and reliable way. Presumably, such intelligent mechanical behavior could be extended into a range of other applications.

The ideal characteristic of artificial intelligence is its ability to rationalize and take actions that have the best chance of achieving a specific goal. Machine learning is a subset of artificial intelligence that refers to the concept that computer programs can automatically learn from and adapt to new data without being assisted by humans. Deep learning techniques enable this automatic learning through the absorption of huge amounts of unstructured data such as text, images, or video material.

Among scientific researchers, interest in AI has gone through a series of waves of expectation and accompanying fears. Now that machines play a significant role in industry, medicine, and technology, the benefits seem to far outweigh the disadvantages. Despite the breakthrough that a neural network–based system can learn to play chess from scratch and outwit highly skilled players, and despite the fact that self-driving cars will be commonplace within a few years, there is no immediate prospect that machines are going to take over from humans or that computer (or robotic) intelligence will surpass human wisdom.

Specialists in this field, like Stuart Russell (2019) of the University of California, Berkeley, have warned of potential existential risks. Russell has set up the Center for Human-Compatible AI to align such technology so that it benefits rather than undermines human advancement. As with so many other technological developments of our time, the critical issues seem to be who will be exercising control and what guidelines they will follow. More specifically, how will we integrate values, feelings, emotions, the creative mind, and the spiritual psyche with such advances? To date, AI thrives on the basis of computational capabilities, producing quantifiable outcomes, many of which are immensely useful and can be produced quicker and more effectively than by humans. This happens, however, without the accompanying enrichment of the human capacities of imagination, intuition, and creativity.

If research into AGI produces sufficiently intelligent software, it might be able to reprogram and improve itself. The improved software might well be able to improve; its intelligence could increase exponentially, even to a degree that could surpass humans. At this moment in time, nobody can predict what future course AGI will take (see Ord 2020, 140–51). The chances are that it will serve our evolution constructively rather than destructively, but, as already indicated, that will depend on who is handling the evolving process, what values are being adopted, what sense of power is being accrued, and who discerns the appropriate moral and ethical values.

The ongoing development of AGI will certainly affect the consciousness of the future and its influence on human behavior at a range of different levels. Will religion/spirituality feature in this process and, if so, to what degree? The answer will determine whether or not the process is imbued with those values that help to protect human integrity and the sacredness of all life forms within creation's web of life.

The Contemplative Gaze

Moving from the technological sphere, where so much energy is focused outwardly, I now turn to the deep, inner realm, specifically to the notion of contemplation. In the Christian tradition contemplation tends to be defined as a content-free mind directed toward the awareness of

God as a living reality, a direct awareness of the divine that transcends the intellect, often in accordance with our meditation. Traditionally, it denotes a way of being that takes one out of the world, although we still remain in it. Erroneously, this has often reinforced the dualistic split between the scared and the secular.

Twentieth-century Cistercian monk Thomas Merton advocated for a more integrated and empowering understanding of contemplation. Merton considered contemplation, not as a privileged grace for the few called to exceptional holiness, but as "the highest expression of man's intellectual and spiritual life. It is that life itself, fully awake, fully active" (Merton 1961, 1). Merton goes on to describe the experience as a knowledge too deep to be grasped in images, words, or even clear concepts. In other words, contemplation is the attainment of another level of consciousness leading to a deeper integration of life and faith.

Merton inspired a new wave of contemplative engagement with life transcending the earlier narrow focus on the human soul that aspired to escape the world for a transcendent union with God in the otherworldly heavenly realm. Links with a more ancient mystical tradition also arise here and have been explored in seminal works by the monastic scholar Bernard McGinn (1991) and contemporary writers such as Douglas Christie (2013) and Beverly Lanzetta (2018). This contemplative dimension is a central feature of eco-spirituality.

Douglas Christie describes contemplative ecology as "an expression of the diverse and wide-ranging desire emerging within contemporary culture to identify our deepest feeling for the natural world as part of a spiritual longing" (Christie 2013, 3). In one inspiring passage Christie writes, "The contemplative's daily attentiveness, alertness, and eagerness of the senses turned outward, help rescue the world from oblivion, even as the contemplative is saved by the simple beauty of the world, by the recognition that the fabric is whole and we are woven deeply into it" (Christie 2013, 56).[3] Such sentiments bring the notion of contemplation into close alliance with the sense of cosmic consciousness outlined above. The consciousness itself is a kind of allurement into the living mystery we name as God, and that mystery is not merely transcendent in the sense of being beyond the material creation. This living mystery is deeply insinuated into it. In and through God's creation we come to know, love, and serve the creator more intimately. Such a contemplative gaze informs and even transforms the quality of our attention and the direction of our intentionality and desiring. Synthesizing ecology and liberation theology, Brazilian theologian Leonardo Boff writes, "The mystic is not detached from history, but committed to it as transformation, starting from a nucleus of transcendent meaning and a minimal utopian dimension which, in as much as it is religious, enables the mystic to be more perceptive than anyone else" (1995, 70).

Thus far in this chapter we have been creating a new vocabulary for the elements and formative stages of eco-spirituality. The basic human experience of being aware, and the desires and intentions arising therefrom, seem to be insinuated into a consciousness that permeates the entire creation and is fundamentally sacred at its core. Those long-cherished notions in the history of spirituality, namely,

---

[3] The development of such contemplation—with the senses turned outward—is further enhanced by contemporary research in microbial ecology, the intricate complex underground interaction of millions of tiny organisms, creating and sustaining the vitality of life. See the inspiring read *Entangled Life* (Sheldrake 2020).

contemplation and mysticism, enable us to unravel something of the deep meaning mediated through the conscious
creation. It is beginning to feel as if all creation might be
viewed as a contemplative ecology (Von Essen 2010).

A New Theological Horizon

Such spiritual reflections invite us to probe deeper and ask
what might be the theological implications of such a spiritual
consciousness now understood to be spread throughout
the entire creation. How might we understand the God,
the creative life-force, at work in it all? John Caputo offers an intriguing option, writing, "I do not take the name
of God to be the name of a being, of an existent, but of
a way I have been overtaken by the world" (2015, 179).
Are we overtaken by a consciousness that is fundamentally
divine? Who or what is the source and well-spring of such
consciousness?

In the 1980s British physicist Paul Davies claimed that
science opened up a surer way to God than mainline religion (Davies 1983). Davies can rightly be criticized for
viewing religion in the narrow doctrinal manner that has
been marginalizing many people in recent decades. His
understanding of science, however, merits our attention.
He embraces many of the key tenets of quantum physics,
viewing energy, radiation, magnetism, waves, and field
theories in a much broader light than conventionally understood. Although he may not be aware of the fact that
recent theological investigations speak of the Holy Spirit in
surprisingly similar terms—energy, radiation, space, force,
field, and light—he would certainly welcome the ensuing
synthesis that has been around since the 1970s.

One of the first contemporary theologians to address this confluence was British scholar Thomas F. Torrance (1972), but the limelight was stolen by German scholar Wolfhart Pannenberg, who, that same year, embraced the connection between theology's understanding of the Holy Spirit and the scientific notion of field influence at work in the natural world (Pannenberg 1972). Pannenberg did not elaborate at length on this new fertile synthesis between science and theology, however, until the publication of volume 2 of *Systematic Theology* in 1994.[4]

Of course some of the great scientists several years previously had already paved the way for this new understanding of the Spirit's creativity at work in the heart of the natural world. In 1936, Albert Einstein wrote, "Everybody who is seriously involved in the pursuit of science becomes convinced that a spirit is manifest in the laws of the universe—a spirit vastly superior to that of mankind, and one in the face of which we with our modest powers must feel humble" (Einstein 1936). And Max Planck, one of the founding fathers of quantum theory, said in 1944:

"All matter originates and exists only by virtue of a force that brings the parts of the atom in vibration, and keeps the smallest solar system of the universe together. So must we assume behind this force the existence of a conscious intelligent spirit. This spirit

---

[4] Meanwhile, another German theologian, Jürgen Moltmann (1985), endorsed the emerging confluence between science and theology. Finally in 2009, German scholar Wolfgang Vondey suggested that the heart of pneumatology after Einstein is located in a different cosmological framework constituted by the notions of order, rationality, relationality, symmetry, and movement (Vondey 2009).

is the basis of all matter. . . . Without spirit, matter wouldn't exist at all—immortal spirit is the truth."[5]

Another German physicist, Hans-Peter Dürr, asserted: "As a physicist, I have spent fifty years—my entire life as a researcher—to ask, what it is that hides behind the material. And the result is simple: There is no matter; basically there is only Spirit" (Dürr 2010, 44). Leonardo Boff is well-justified, therefore, in providing us with this observation: "To fully understand the Spirit, we need a different paradigm, more in line with modern cosmology. The energy that upholds the universe, and all the beings that have been and will be, penetrates creation from beginning to end" (2015, viii).

As already indicated in Chapter 3, the religious appropriation of this inspiring scientific wisdom is nowhere more real than in the notion of the Great Spirit, adopted by Indigenous Peoples all over our world (O'Murchu 2011). For these peoples we discern and connect with the living spirit, in and through the land, the soil, the creative energy of our earthiness, the clay out of which all life is formed. Canadian theologian Norman Wirzba extends that same convivial relationship with the land into Christian discipleship for the twenty-first century (Wirzba 2022).

In mainline Christianity that same conviction might be formulated through Teilhard de Chardin's observation that love is the affinity which links and draws together the elements of the world, an agent of universal synthesis, the free and imaginative outpouring of the Spirit, over all unexplored paths. Unfortunately, Christians have tended

---

[5] Planck said this in a speech he gave in Florence, Italy, in 1944, entitled "Das Wesen der Materie" (The Nature of Matter).

to reserve such love to humans and, uniquely, for their relationship with the more personalized God. In many cases
people feel they can only access such love after they have
endured pain and suffering to "make up" to God for their
sinfulness and wayward behavior.

Eco-spirituality, on the other hand, seeks to move us
beyond the guilt trip and the widespread devotional need
to pacify God—thus averting God's anger—so that God
will love us. Eco-spirituality moves beyond the anthropocentric personalism to the transpersonal realm, wherein we
understand human growth and flourishing to be integral
to the growth and flourishing of creation at large (Wirzba
2022). As earthlings, we cannot grow into the fullness of
life (Jn 10:10) without bringing the earth and all creation
with us. More accurately, this transformative growth happens as the creative energy of the Great Spirit renews and
invigorates our earthly becoming.

In this approach consciousness can be explained as the
love of God poured out in energizing empowerment for
everything in creation, humans included. The dualistic
split between sacred and secular has no place in this divine
synthesis; neither is there any room for any one species
lording it over all others. We are together in this energizing transformative process wherein all are growing and
evolving, or none are.

The Obstacles We Need to Confront

Are these new horizons of consciousness for everybody
or merely for the select few—the scientific geniuses of our
age, and those privileged with contemplative wisdom? Because we live in a world of mass information—and such
information is an energy form ultimately energized by the

Holy Spirit of God—the chances are that all are invited to embrace these new expanded and inspiring horizons. Possibly millions are already being lured along, with most largely unaware of what is actually transpiring.

Such an awakening of consciousness is particularly acute for those in our world still operating out of imperial ideologies, that functional level of awareness that continues to treat everything in creation as an object for human use, and humans as the only intelligent beings entitled to lord it over all else. The addiction to patriarchal power, more than anything else, holds our world to ransom and blocks the flow of the awakening consciousness described in this chapter.[6] Unfortunately, many major world religions also play significantly into the maintenance and promotion of such imperial consciousness.

In light of the above observations more and more people are feeling a sense of unease (dis-ease?) with formal churches and religions. Instead, they are hungering for those deeper and more expansive horizons described by modern spirituality. For mainline religionists there is something authentic about religion in the face of which spirituality is questionable, dubious, and unreliable. The perception and conviction seem to be that, if we take religion seriously and practice it as the official sources suggest, then we don't need spirituality. The perception seems to be that spirituality is a distraction from the "real thing."

---

[6] This is obvious in such developments as the ideologies of Donald Trump in the United States, of Boris Johnson in the UK, and of Jair Bolsonaro in Brazil. It reveals a more violent face in Vladimir Putin's attack on Ukraine, or in the oppression of the military regimes in Myanmar and North Korea. That same hunger for raw power drives several violent groups across Africa and elsewhere on our planet.

Throughout much of Christian history a distinction pre-vailed between the public and the private spheres. Liturgy, or formal worship, was generally perceived as the best way to be true to one's religion. Since preaching and teaching took place within the context of worship, these provided the resources and guidelines to live better religious lives. On the other hand, every major world religion has a private, devotional aspect, the practice of which is guided by the religion but frequently left to the devotees' own initiative. Typically, this includes prayer formulas such as novenas (to appease or convince God); ascetical practices such as fasting, employment of statues, icons, or other holy objects; devotional home altars or shrines; and pilgrimages. Occasionally the public and private come together, as in the popular fiestas found in several religious traditions.

Such devotional practices still play a major role in maintaining the imperial tenor of faith and religion. While needed by the millions of impoverished people who cry out each day for God's mercy—and need to do so simply to survive in the face of often appalling conditions—such devotions are a major obstacle to the deeper integration envisaged by the eco-spirituality explored in this book. Typically, such devotions create a strong sense of co-dependency, looking to the authority of God and that of humans to rescue us from life's misfortunes. Such cultures of devotion are heavily anthropocentric and contribute little to the integration of the human with the rest of creation.

Since most readers of this book are likely to be from a Christian background, they face what is both a sensitive and complex challenge. Our Christian faith carries a great deal of imperial baggage. We see it very clearly in the foundational sources of our faith, as illustrated by the Greek theologian Francesca Stavrakopoulou:

Scholars have long suspected that El, not Yahweh, was the original God of the people known in the Bible as "Israel." Yahweh would gradually come to usurp his father El. But quite how this happened is frustratingly unclear. It is possible that the transition was tied to the socio-political conditions that gave rise to the emergence of the kingdoms of Israel and Judah early in the first millennium BCE. With kingship and statecraft came ideologies of militarized power—and the need for kings to exhibit themselves as warriors endorsed by fearsome divine fighters. As a storm God, Yahweh was naturally a God of warfare, equipped with weapons of thunder, lightning and rain clouds, and it was Yahweh's personal patronage the kings of Israel and Judah claimed. . . . Yahweh would come to be presented as a God intolerant of other deities, and Yahweh worship would become increasingly mono-latrous. (Stavrakopoulou 2021, 22, 25)

That imperialistic sense of God and religion is fragmenting in our time and leaving us with a disturbing vacuum that spirituality seeks to fill through a complex—and at times confusing—set of articulations. Eco-spirituality takes the exploration to even greater depths, seeking, above all else, a renewed integration between humans and creation and a deep desire to transform inherited dysfunctional power games into a new empowering synthesis for humans and Planet Earth alike.

The Way Ahead

Throughout the latter half of the twentieth century, and into the opening decades of the present century, spirituality became ever more disconnected from formal religion, producing a vast range of studies overviewed in works such as Lucy Bregman's *The Ecology of Spirituality* (2014). Among the features of the emerging spirituality, the following require and deserve a deeper analysis and a more informed sense of discernment.

1. Spirituality as a precursor to formal religion, recapitulating a spiritual consciousness that has been unfolding over several thousands of years.
2. Spirituality as a force for integration long predating the divisive distinctions of dualistic thinking, particularly the split between the sacred and the secular.
3. The need to unravel the power at work in several forms of popular religiosity and move our discernment in the direction of empowerment (power with) rather than patriarchal domination (power over).

No analysis of contemporary spirituality would be complete without acknowledging this shift in consciousness away from power from on high and toward empowerment from the center outward. All major religions, not merely Christianity, are wrapped up in power structures that are no longer credible today. More important, they do not seem to have been either relevant or useful in the long historical development of spirituality outlined in the present work. Attending to consciousness through the shift to larger horizons of awareness, with the need to give more discerning attention and intention to all we do and undertake, eco-spirituality offers a valuable corrective. This more egalitarian consciousness of our time tends to be critical of the various modes of power and domination at work in our world. Indeed, we live at a time when millions are highly suspicious of all forms of authority from the top down, with a deep distrust of how such power is exercised in both secular and religious spheres. Eco-spirituality can empower us as we heal the many relationships broken by dominance.

Critical Issues for Ongoing Discernment

1. "Consciousness isn't something we have; it's what we and the whole world are" (Currivan 2017, 233).
2. The contemporary scientific study of consciousness complements and enriches our understanding of the energy of the Holy Spirit at work throughout creation, as a life-force that is fundamentally benign and empowering.
3. Consciousness can be explained as the love of God poured out in energizing empowerment for everything in creation, humans included. The dualistic split between sacred and secular has no place in this divine synthesis.
4. Consciousness alerts us to the intelligent wisdom at work in creation's evolving process, not to be narrowly reduced to intelligent machines (as in AGI), but understood as a spiritual endowment of all creation.
5. In eco-spirituality, contemplation today is better understood as a deeper alignment with the emerging consciousness of our time: "the diverse and wide-ranging desire emerging within contemporary culture to identify our deepest feeling for the natural world as part of a spiritual longing" (Christie 2013, 3).
6. "The contemplative's daily attentiveness, alertness, and eagerness of the senses turned outward, help rescue the world from oblivion, even as the contemplative is saved by the simple beauty of the world, by the recognition that the fabric is whole and we are woven deeply into it" (Christie 2013, 56).

7. "To fully understand the Spirit, we need a different paradigm, more in line with modern cosmology. The energy that upholds the universe, and all the beings that have been and will be, penetrates creation from beginning to end" (Boff 2015, viii).

9

Eco-Spirituality and
Christian Foundations

*Christology is creation underlined, concentrated
and condensed; Faith in creation as God wishes
it to be.*

—EDWARD SCHILLEBEECKX

*A Christology deaf to the cries of the world is
unable to utter any divine Word.*

—RAIMON PANIKKAR

For much of the Christian era the spiritual life carried a
dual significance. There were those who were called to the
way of perfection: monks, hermits, nuns, and, above all
else, priests, long considered to be God's primary repre-
sentatives on earth. Likewise, there were those who have
often been described as the ordinary people, long viewed as
passive recipients of the grace of holiness mediated through
the church, its sacraments, and particularly its priests as
preachers and teachers of truth.

The dualistic splitting often referenced in this book is all
too obvious in this divided and divisive portrayal of holiness. There are those who have privileged access to holiness

(spirituality), called forth and mandated by the church to provide the people with the wherewithal through which they can escape this world and attain to the fulfillment of heaven in a life hereafter.

In the other half of the dualistic split are the powerless masses, victims of original sin, fundamentally flawed in a sin-corrupted creation. Only an authentic spiritual life that consists of prayer, penance, allegiance to the patriarchal church (and its sacramental system), and unquestioned obedience to the church and its teaching authority reassures devotees that they stood some chance of making it through to the promise of eternal salvation.

The Shifting Foundations

Millions of Christians around the world, particularly those of older years or adherents of more fundamentalist strands of contemporary Christianity, will easily recognize this rather negative, divisive portrayal. Some will rightly claim that it is something of a caricature, that it was never as bad as that, and that despite its limitations, millions grew through it and some in spite of it, into being wholesome people of faith whose influence on the world at large was graceful and transformative. Others will want me to move away from this negative portrayal since it is no longer prevalent, as growing numbers of people today have already outgrown it and left it behind. It is viewed as a baggage from the past, a kind of primitive way of understanding God and the world, that has no place in the more advanced wisdom of the twenty-first century.[1]

---

[1] I suggest it is more appropriate—and responsible—to argue that it is no longer meaningful within the evolutionary consciousness of

In conjunction with contemporary Christian discernment and the scholarly approach of our time deemed more suitable for sacred learning, I wish to adopt a strategy of reworking the tradition. Within an evolutionary context, we, as a spiritually informed species, learn as we go along. In our long evolutionary story of some seven million years, we seem to have gotten it right most of the time because we remained very close to nature. We have also gotten it badly wrong some of the time, as in the post-Constantine imperialism that dominated Christianity for over fifteen-hundred years. Therefore, from within the Christian context itself, I want to rework the tradition at four levels:

1. The liberating and empowering spirituality of Jesus and the Gospels before it was dislodged by Constantine and the imperial contagion of subsequent centuries;

2. The Pre-Constantinian period—up to approximately 300 CE—a period of complex evolution of faith and spirituality that has long been suppressed and ignored but is now being retrieved in contemporary research with substantial implications for the vision of eco-spirituality being outlined in the present work;

3. The eco-spiritual reawakening of the Middle Ages, when the enclosure of monasticism gave way to new engagements with God's creation, accompanied with a fresh mystical awakening and an eco-feminism that has been largely neglected in Christian history; and

4. The impact of modern science, particularly cosmology and the earth sciences, alerting us to a sense

---

the twenty-first century as named by contemporary scholars such as Ilia Delio, John Haught, and Carter Phipps.

of mystery within the evolution of creation itself; this awakening sense of mystery has contributed to a newly evolving synthesis between creation and spirituality, for which the Earth Charter serves as an inspiring example. I will briefly review its challenges for eco-spirituality.

Spirituality of the Upside Down Kingdom

Since the late 1800s, scripture scholars have highlighted a strand of gospel discernment that was not merely neglected but actually suppressed for much of the two-thousand years of Christendom, namely, the notion of the *kingdom of God* and its central role in the life and ministry of the historical Jesus. The dislocation and suppression of this key concept seems to have been caused by the imperial understanding of divine kingship, which predates both Judaism and Christianity, but was largely, if not totally, rejected by the historical Jesus.[2]

I have covered this topic in a number of previous works (O'Murchu 2017; 2021), and here I will offer a rather general overview. Most important, I support the desire among a growing number of scripture scholars to move away from imperial language related to kings and kingdoms and instead use language that is likely to better represent what Jesus desired in the liberation and empowerment of gospel faith. To that end I tend to use the Aramaic-related translation *companionship of empowerment*. When it comes such

---

[2] The renowned Catholic scholar John P. Meier (d. 2022) claims that the term *kingdom of God* is employed by Jesus in the gospel narratives in a way that has few if any precedents within Judaism or in any of the ancient religious sources predating Christianity (see Meier 1994).

renaming, I support John Dominic Crossan's encouragement to do our homework on the new understanding that Jesus seems to have desired and adopt novel namings (relevant language) for the diverse cultural contexts we encounter (Crossan 2022).[3]

Of the two key words, *companionship* is the more revolutionary. It denotes mutuality and community. Of course, *empowerment* could be activated by a benign king. My contention, however, is that Jesus would not be interested in any kind of king, benign or otherwise. He wanted an end to all forms of kingship, replacing the structure with a whole new empowering dynamic based on mutual participation and interdependence. He wanted every pyramid replaced with a circle and every hierarchy yielding pride of place to the holarchical structure evidenced throughout creation.[4]

The companionship of empowerment makes a double shift: from power over to power with, and from unilateral domination to communal collaboration (Crossan 2010). It marks a seismic shift from exclusivity to radical inclusiveness. As in our time, so also in the time of Jesus, the royal dispensation was heavily couched in elitism and exclusion.

---

[3] "God's kingdom was to be the final fulfillment of biblical dreams for a world of distributive justice, the ideal realization of biblical hopes for a world of cosmic nonviolence, and the climax of biblical promises for a world of universal peace. . . . The specific phrase 'Kingdom of God' is practically non-existent prior to Jesus' usage. So, a good translation should offer some hint as to why Jesus invented it as his own favorite designation for a transformed world and a transfigured earth" (Crossan 2022, 282).

[4] Biologists frequently reference nested hierarchies that they detect throughout creation. I suspect that such observations arise from their academic conditioning, and thus they see what they expect to see—a kind of self-fulfilling prophesy. For the holarchical understanding of creation, see Jude Currivan (2017).

Royal patronage was often reserved to specific families, and within the exercise of kingly power only the privileged few obtained close access. The king's palace was heavily forti- fied, and admission was only allowed to an elite. Opulence and glory befitted royal accolade, far in excess of what the ordinary people could ever hope to experience. A vast chasm stood between the king and the people.

The historical Jesus, however, seems to have declared an end to such imperial exclusion. Wendy Farley expresses this breakthrough well: "In this empire (kingdom of God) neither victims nor perpetrators find the door slammed in their faces. . . . If we accept its healing, we are asked to accept that everyone else in the entire world is a citizen of this Kingdom" (Farley 2011, 204). In the companionship of empowerment, nobody is out, and therefore, everybody is included. Power and privilege are no longer reserved to the select few. The pyramid has been transfigured into a circle. Animation is activated from the center outward in an embrace that excludes no one. The "privileges" of this new dispensation belong primarily to those who have never known anything but exclusion: the poor, the marginalized, the despised, and the disenfranchised. The companionship of empowerment is an upside-down kingdom (Kraybill 1990).

John Shelby Spong claims that Paul's extensive use of the notion of righteousness, frequently used in the Letter to the Romans, may be considered an equivalent to the gospel notion of the kingdom of God, with the central focus on right relating, in the name of love, justice, liberation, and empowerment (Spong 2016, 134).

The kingdom of God comes when we are empowered to live fully, to love wastefully and to be all that we are capable of being. It means that the work of the kingdom of God is the work of enhancing human wholeness. . . . It means that the work of the kingdom of God is done when the eyes of the blind are opened to see reality undistorted by religious propaganda and the ears of the deaf are opened to listen to truth even when it threatens our religious security. It means that the limbs of the twisted, the crippled and the broken will be able to leap with joy as new humanity breaks in upon us without the distortions of our tribal past. It means that the voices of those once muted by fear can sing as they watch all the life-denying prejudices that separate human beings into destructive camps fade away and die. That will be the time when the kingdom of God becomes visible, and that will be when God's righteousness—for which, without always knowing it, human beings have both hungered and thirsted—will finally be revealed. (Spong 2016, 140)

Thus far I am emphasizing the significance of this new companionship for people, our relationship with God and with one another, cast in a radical new mode of inclusivity, empowerment, and liberation. However, it seems that Jesus did not intend this new dispensation to be for humans only. He envisaged a call to discipleship that would include the entire creation. Consider the following descriptions from three contemporary scholars:

If separation is not the ideal, but connection is; if dualism is not the ideal but the relational embrace of diversity is; if hierarchy is not the ideal but mutuality is; then the kinship model more closely approximates reality. It sees human beings and the earth with all its creatures intrinsically related as companions in a community of life. Because we are all mutually interconnected, the flourishing or damaging of one ultimately affects all. (Johnson 1993, 30)[5]

The rule of God refers to the intention of the Creator, the way God desires creation to be, especially human existence in a community that includes relationship with the wider life of the planet. . . . The rule of God represents no small insight. It symbolizes being drawn into the mystery of God's intention for the universe. . . . It opens up a framework of how human beings should live and what they should live for in this world. (Haight 2019, 214)

Jesus of Nazareth proclaimed the "reign of God" in accordance with the pattern of the religion of creation, while denouncing the religion of empire as a demonic counterfeit. (Howard-Brook 2016, xiii)

These three statements clearly assert that, for Jesus, the new companionship was never intended for humans only, and less so for the salvation of human souls in a world hereafter. To the contrary, it embraces the entire cosmic and planetary creation, evoking a new horizon in which an authentic human relationship with God is only possible in and through a radically new way of relating with every aspect of the

---

[5] More recently Elizabeth Johnson has written: "Since the reign of God is especially attentive to the needy and outcast, Jesus showed a partisanship for suffering people that we can today interpret as extending to encompass the earth and its myriads of distressed species and ecosystems. His ministry reveals a wideness in God's mercy that includes all creation" (Johnson 2018, 82).

creation we inhabit. From a Christian perspective, this is the most robust foundation we can ever hope for in terms of eco-spirituality.

Franciscan theologian Ilia Delio helps us understand how being more inclusive of the wider web of life illuminates the mystery of the Godhead itself to a degree largely, if not totally, unknown in all previous Christian attempts at an understanding of theodicy. Delio declares quite unambiguously: "Creation is not a backdrop for human drama but the disclosure of God's identity" (Delio 2011, 13). The frequent assertions in John's Gospel of Jesus being at one with the will and desire of the Father must now be heard in a transpersonal mode of discernment that is inclusive of all creation and not merely a reflection of how a person relates with a father-like figure.

Eco-spirituality is foundational to the enlarged understanding of God and life inscribed in our Christian faith and, indeed, in every major world religion. How, then, did we miss this expanded vision, and for so long? Franciscan spiritual guide Richard Rohr is right in suggesting that our restricted cosmology is at the root of the problem. "Our faith became a competitive theology, with various parochial theories of salvation, instead of a universal cosmology inside of which all can live with an inherent dignity" (Rohr 2019, 17). This enlarged Christian horizon quickly became compromised and subverted as the Christian faith came under the influence of Roman imperialism, particularly from the time of Constantine onward. The evolution of the Christian faith between 50 CE and 300 CE, however, is another, largely subverted, horizon that further illuminates the challenges we face in developing a contemporary eco-spirituality.

The Long-Neglected
Early Tradition

In the remarkable *After Jesus, Before Christianity*, Erin
Vearncombe, Bernard Brandon Scott, Hal Taussig, and Sue
Monk Kidd have closely reexamined what was transpiring within and around the Christian faith during the two
decades following the death and resurrection of Jesus. In
broad strokes they review the historical and religious developments happening from the middle of the first century
until the beginning of the fourth century, when the Roman
Emperor Constantine paved the way for the incorporation
of Christianity into the Roman Empire.

I have already highlighted the imperial consciousness
within which the notion of the kingdom of God was in-
terpreted, depicting Jesus as a faithful, obedient servant
of God understood as a ruling king. Through obedience
even to the point of death, Jesus upheld and pursued God's
desire to rescue the world from the forces of sin and evil.
True discipleship in this mode is widely understood as loyal
obedience and submission from the designated leaders of
faith, purported to be in direct succession to Peter and the
other apostles. In time, that leadership came to be identified
with popes, bishops, and especially priests.

As Vearncombe et al. (2022, 33–96) demonstrate, how
such patriarchal leadership evolved is now understood to be
immensely more complex, uncertain, and varied than what
we have long assumed. Discipleship in the Gospels has been
over identified with the twelve apostles (about whom we
know very little). Luke also references the seventy-two,
and strands of female leadership, especially around Mary
Magdalene, also prevailed. It has also been suggested that
the central role of the Twelve may be more symbolic,

representing the Twelve Tribes of Israel with Jesus viewed as the new Moses, than factual.

Additionally, there is the growing concern about the Acts of the Apostles and its largely exaggerated and inflated account of early Christian history. It would seem that Luke has reassembled the Twelve to lay a solid "ecclesiastical" foundation for his two big heroes, Peter and Paul. It seems that the Twelve were dispersed after the untimely death of Jesus lest they too be crucified. To suggest that they all came back pushes credulity to limits that are increasingly difficult to accept.

These arguments lead to a long-neglected historical and ecclesial question: Who actually laid the foundations for the post-resurrection faith community? We have long assumed it was Peter and the Twelve, literalizing the second chapter of Acts, but the only person named in the Gospels to receive a post-resurrection apostolic commission is Mary Magdalene (Jn 20:17). Might she not be the primordial disciple, with her cohort of women and men, laying the foundations of what today we call the church? In concluding his Letter to the Romans, for example, Paul highlights the several women who were involved in the early Christian movement.

According to the historian Mary Malone (2014), female leadership was at the fore in the early decades of the Christian movement and began to fade from around 55 CE onward, as a male-dominated church began to emerge. I am much more attracted to the assessment of biblical scholar James Carroll (2014), who suggests that this female-led movement continued to grow and expand up to the mid/late 60s, until it was undermined and dislodged by the Jewish-Roman War of 66–72 CE. War wreaked havoc on women's initiative, as warfare has been doing throughout the centuries.

Until that time, with the war culminating in the destruction of the Jerusalem Temple, there was no clear-cut distinction between Jews and Christians. Both subscribed to Jewish ways of life, with a quality of tolerance and mutuality that is difficult for us moderns to understand or appreciate. Moreover, there was a great deal of diversity, including tolerance for different understandings of God and divine worship (see Ehrman 2018; Vearncombe et al. 2022). After the war and the dissolution of the Temple, the two groups began to separate, but probably not with the religious bigotry and division that historians have emphasized.

The Jewish people, through their leaders, restructured their faith, replacing the Temple with the Torah—the first five books of the Bible. They adopted the Torah as the Law of God that would guide them from there on. Their focus on law was not entirely legalistic, as a complementary form of wisdom and interpretation began to surface. It is known as *Midrash*. According to the Jewish scholar Jacob Neusner (2014), Midrash is a Jewish mode of interpretation that was prevalent for the first six centuries of the Christian era, focusing on paraphrase, prophesy, and parable, engaging afresh the words of the text while also interpreting behind the text and beyond it. Midrash opens up the possibility for various interpretations that are applicable to a range of life experiences.

Meanwhile, after the destruction of the Temple in 70 CE, the First and Second Letters of Timothy indicate that the Christians became more institutional and clericalized, and we begin to see negative reaction to the female presence and contribution to church life. As Judaism evolved, Christians also adopted informal strategies and structures that have been largely neglected in Christian history. For instance, the Eucharist meal adopted the structure of the

Jewish Shabbat meal, with women playing the key role, as illustrated by Osiek and MacDonald (2007). Even when numbers grew larger and Christians adopted the banquet format, following Greek and Roman practice, the mutually empowering structure of agape love feasts seems to have been employed, sometimes with the equivalent of an ordained priest facilitating, and, at other times, a range of other persons facilitating. Vearncombe et al. (2022) claim that this extensive and diverse sense of flexibility, variety, and creativity prevailed well into the 200s. The ecclesiastical conformity that has been so much emphasized in Christian history is largely a post-Constantinian development that did not become obvious till the late 400s.

What relevance does all this have for eco-spirituality? These early Christian centuries were marked by a distinctive anti-imperial, postcolonial counterculture, a kind of "people power" from the ground up, facilitated through a range of small groups, associations, and anti-imperial networks (Vearncombe et al. 2022). Although this egalitarian spirit was centered mainly on people and their desire to overthrow foreign colonization, it also embraced a range of ecological concerns. The long-held conviction that the land was God's primary gift to the people inspired several attempts to protect the land and reclaim it from the greed and usurpation of Roman land grabbing. A significant feature of the people's sense of self-reliance was based on their ability to grow much of their own food in the family garden and rely on a range of herbs for medicinal and health purposes.

Throughout these early centuries men and women collaborated quite closely, devoid of the misogyny that prevailed under later imperial governance. Justice for humans and for all other creatures (eco-justice) would not have been as clearly demarcated as we see today, but that value orientation was much more prevalent than has been acknowledged by mainline historians. Foundationally, the fluidity and flexibility of those early centuries inculcated a way of life in which many of the key values and virtues of eco-spirituality were naturally and organically integrated.

Finally, despite the fact that various groups continued to dislodge Roman invasion by adopting violent means, it seems that a culture of nonviolence was a live option for early Christians (Rynne 2008). In part, we see this exemplified in the iconography of the Catacombs in Rome, where we would expect images of crosses and crucifixions but instead see a predominance of images of nature, luscious green pastures with an array of birds and animals. Apparently those early martyrs did not view their untimely deaths in terms of escaping to a faraway heavenly realm, instead understanding their deaths as a contribution to bringing about heaven on earth, recreating paradise within the realm of God's creation (Brock and Parker, 2008).

Reawakening of the Middle Ages

Often described by historians as a dark age of the church, including the devastating impact of the Black Death in the fourteenth century, the period between 1100 CE and 1400 CE produced a remarkable reawakening of earth-centered faith characterized by many of the outstanding features we associate with eco-spirituality today. The great St. Francis of Assisi is often the first called to mind, with his apostolic zeal for the poor and marginalized and his deep love for nature, for Brother Sun and Sister Moon, and for the radiance of God visible in all created life.

Less well known are the outstanding mystical giants of the Middle Ages, particularly:

- *Hildegarde of Bingen* (1098–1179) was an extraordinary, multi-gifted woman, whose poetry, music, painting, and writing continue to inspire right up to the present. Her sense of "greening" faith and theology is often invoked in the eco-spiritual revival of our time.
- *Mechtild of Magdeburg* (1210–80) was a Beguine[6] for most of her life, and she sought to address the corruption within the church, incurring much criticism for her efforts. Her compassionate love for life embraced all creation. Her deep hunger for justice toward women morphed into a desire for eco-justice for all life forms threatened, oppressed, or ignored.
- *Meister Eckhart* (1260–1329) was condemned after his death by the church, probably in part because of his support for the Beguines. As a creation-centered mystic, Eckhart's writings reveal an intense sense of the presence of God in all living things, thus making the natural world a mirror radiating and reflecting God's love and goodness (Fox 2014).
- *Julian of Norwich* (1342–1415) was a British mystic and champion for the notion of the motherhood of God. Belonging to the later Middle Ages, she followed very much in the vein of the other outstanding names listed above. In the wake of the Black Death she kept alive an enduring sense of courage and hope amid the prevalent despondency of that time.

---

[6] Beguines were groups of women who lived lives of prayer and service in community but did not join an approved religious order and were not subject to clerical oversight.

- *Thomas Aquinas* (1225–74), although widely known as a theological giant, provided enduring inspiration for the evolving mystical and creation-based movements of his day. His contribution to a more holistic, post-dualistic sense of Christian spirituality is a contribution for which he deserves a great deal of credit (Fox 2020). The following are just two oft-cited quotes that highlight Aquinas's revelation of God within the cosmic creation: "For each one in its nature is good, but all together are very good, on account of the order of the universe, which is the ultimate and noblest perfection in things" (Aquinas 2010, c45.9). "The whole universe together participates in the divine goodness and represents it better than any single being whatsoever." (Aquinas 1911–25, Ia, q.47, a.1).[7]

Recapitulation in the Twenty-First Century

Despite the long history of dualistic splitting between secular and sacred, between earth and heaven, body and spirit, Christianity has never entirely lost sight of the centrality of the cosmos and the love of God revealed in the unfolding of creation at large. In the latter half of the twentieth

---

[7] Matthew Fox, more than anybody else, has helped to popularize and make accessible to a general audience the mystical dimensions of creation spirituality. Best known is his *Original Blessing* (Fox 1983). I also recommend his *Christian Mystics* (Fox 2011). Advocates of creation theology/spirituality would also expect me to highlight others from within the Christian tradition supporting the central role of creation in our theological and spiritual understanding of faith. These include Australian theologian Denis Edwards (2017), for whom St. Bonaventure (1221–74) is of primary significance; and American theologian Daniel P. Horan (2019), for whom John Duns Scotus (1265–1308) is a significant source.

century that same enduring strand of creation spirituality emerged once more. Almost unknown to ourselves, we are reworking the tradition in a discerning process that is both inspiring and driving the enlarged spiritual vision of the present work. It is very much a process of revisiting and reappropriating ancient wisdom to reclaim afresh the richness of ancient wisdom as a resource to propel us, in a more empowering way, toward a new, enlarged future.

This is an evolutionary process, elucidated afresh by many of the great visionaries of the late twentieth century, including Pierre Teilhard de Chardin, Thomas Berry, John F. Haught, and Ilia Delio. That which is often dismissed as postmodernism, perceived as an irresponsible abandonment of the leading metanarratives of the past, on closer examination is a transitional process that brings with it much of the long-buried wisdom of earlier times. Thus my claim throughout this book that spirituality is not a byproduct of formal religion, but rather something that predates religion by several thousands of years. As we go further back into deep time, we begin to notice that spirituality transcends many, if not all, of the dualistic splittings upon which religions have often flourished.

How we personalize our faith is another issue that can be addressed anew in light of this recapitulation of earlier Christian wisdom. In conventional Christian spirituality we are frequently reminded that a personal relationship with God—through Jesus—is paramount to our faith and its integration into our daily lives. In this context the human person is superior to all other lifeforms, for humans alone are ensouled beings. Grounding spiritual meaning in other lifeforms or in the natural world is perceived to be a distraction from or a threat to the personal relationship with the Holy One. In some extreme cases eco-spirituality will be dismissed as a New Age phenomenon, akin to some ancient pagan worship.

In a previous work (O'Murchu 2022) I distinguish between the personal and the transpersonal, and that distinction is crucial to the integration being pursued in contemporary eco-spirituality. The transpersonal—as used today in both Jungian psychology and anthropology—is not about transcending, bypassing, or outgrowing what it means to be human. Rather, it claims that we can only grow into authentic humanhood by being deeply immersed in the material creation, the natural world, out of which we were begotten in the first place; as earthlings and not merely ensouled beings awaiting our fuller realization (salvation) in a life hereafter.

The current emphasis on our identity and role as earthlings is very deep and ancient. It is the kind of identity that prevailed throughout much of our time as hunter-gatherers and, indeed, long before that. But the material of this chapter highlights that it is also an identity that is deeply rooted in the foundational strands of Christian faith and is central to Jesus's own understanding of what the Gospels name as the kingdom of God. Despite the invasive rationality of Hellenization in the early Christian centuries, the growing body of scholarly research today indicates that the early Christians held a more organic, egalitarian understanding of their faith, as we are now rediscovering in our exploration of eco-spirituality (Vearncombe et al. 2022).

Revisiting the Earth Charter

It seems to me that the Earth Charter is a contemporary visionary document that serves aptly for a reappropriation of our Christian tradition for the context of the twenty-first century. I therefore conclude this chapter with an overview of the Earth Charter, highlighting those salient features that are central to the emerging eco-spirituality of this time.

The Earth Charter was initially created in 1987, when the United Nations World Commission on Environment and Development called for a new vision to guide our world in the transition to sustainable development. The first version was compiled by Canadian diplomat Maurice Strong (d. 2015) and then-president of the USSR Mikhail Gorbachev (d. 2022). The drafting of the current text was done during a six-year worldwide consultation process (1994–2000) overseen by the independent Earth Charter Commission, which was convened by Strong and Gorbachev with the purpose of developing a global consensus on values and principles for a sustainable future. The commission continues to serve as the steward of the Earth Charter text.

The following statements from the Earth Charter endorse and reinforce the central values highlighted in the present work.

> 1. *Earth, our home, is alive with a unique community of life. . . . The protection of Earth's vitality, diversity, and beauty is a sacred trust. (Preamble)*

The Earth Charter declares unambiguously that all forms of aliveness are derived from the cosmic-earth context of creation and not merely an endowment unique to humans; that ours is a derived mode of aliveness totally dependent on the "vitality, diversity, and beauty" of the larger organism. As indicated in Chapter 3, this is also a foundational premise of eco-spirituality, with the additional claim that the spiritual dimension seems essential if politics, economics, and social policies are to integrate, protect, and advance such foundational aliveness throughout the entire creation.

2. *Every form of life has value regardless of its worth to human beings. (1a)*

Anthropocentrism—the notion that humans are superior to all creation and that everything else exists for the benefit of human beings—continues to be a stringent ideology, wreaking havoc on all lifeforms, the human itself included. In recent decades our human role in the evolutionary unfolding of life has been subjected to renewed scrutiny as the long-held Christian view of humans as the masters of creation continues to lose credibility and meaning. Nonetheless, a formidable challenge remains for humans to become a servant species rather than a marauding and domineering one. Such a shift in perspective is unlikely without the quality of faith and spirituality outlined in the present work.

3. *Promote the development, adoption, and equitable transfer of environmentally sound technologies. (7c)*

As indicated in Chapter 7, current technological progress will continue apace and may well be the primary driver of evolution throughout the twenty-first century. The benefits to humankind are often lauded, while the impact on the natural world requires a great deal more attention and redress. What is also becoming clearer by the day is that the negative impact upon the earth and its various lifeforms adversely affects human well-being, often quite directly, as in the case of COVID-19 in the early 2020s.

In order to address "the development, adoption, and equitable transfer of environmentally sound technologies," we must create and implement a range of ethical and moral values. This urgent moral imperative will require a great deal of courage and discernment in a current world order that operates within what largely seems to be a moral vacuum. Since religions can no longer provide persuasive and relevant morality—some will argue that it is religion itself that has created the moral vacuity—the challenge becomes a political responsibility for world governments and for our elected parliamentarians. Eco-spirituality stands on quite new ground in advocating such a creation-centered morality for the twenty-first century.

> 4. *Guarantee the right to potable water, clean air, food security, uncontaminated soil, shelter, and safe sanitation, allocating the national and international resources required. (9a)*

Spirituality has long been understood as a resource for lifting people into a more transcendent way of being while providing the wherewithal for this immersion in a more integrated sense of the sacred. To reach such lofty heights, however, spirituality has consistently asked that we give attention to the ordinary things of life and live out of a sense of grace and gratitude. It becomes so much easier to cultivate and sustain our faith in God when the basics of life—water, air, food, soil, shelter, sanitation—are available in a nourishing and empowering way. Above all else, eco-spirituality seeks to celebrate the sacred in the ordinary, inviting us all to outgrow harmful dualisms and become proactive in providing, for all earth-creatures, the basics to live with dignity.

> 5. *Ensure that all trade supports sustainable resource use, environmental protection, and progressive labor standards.* (10c)

Nothing is to be excluded from the purview of eco-spirituality. World trade is not merely a secular task to muster financial gain to the advantage of select groups or sectors of human society. It needs to be seen as a process of sharing earth's resources, benefiting humans in a manner that enhances and protects all the life organisms that are being exchanged. Therefore, world trade practices need to be developed and protected in accordance with life-enhancing moral principles. This requires humans from the fields of politics, economics, social policy, resource management, and cross-cultural marketing, among others, to work collaboratively for the common good of humans and nonhumans alike.

> 6. *Affirm the right of indigenous peoples to their spirituality, knowledge, lands and resources and to their related practice of sustainable livelihoods.* (12b)

Until the mid-1960s the First Nations People of Australia were often categorized as "flora and fauna," judged to be inferior to humans and even to the creatures of the animal kingdom. This crude and cruel suppression has left a legacy of human pain and anguish that has percolated into several spheres of human marginalization. In spiritual terms it has cast millions outside the privileged space of formalized, colonially imposed religion. It has cut off millions of our contemporaries from the rich ancient resources of ancestral wisdom. Currently, it prevents many religionists from studying and incorporating the spiritual richness of Indigenous Peoples around the world.

> 7. *Enhance the role of the mass media in raising awareness of ecological and social challenges. Recognize the importance of moral and spiritual education for sustainable living. (14 c-d)*

Since the mid-twentieth century we have had continuous reminders of a world becoming ever more enthralled with the impact of mass information, with an ever-expanding repertoire of media outlets. Information around the planet is now instantaneous, and many people feel bombarded by information overload. Once again, the benefits are widely documented, but the downside is often neglected. Additionally, new waves of consciousness inundate our lives, changing perceptions, values, and possibilities. Educationally, enough resources have not been devoted to providing the skills so urgently needed for the global transformation to be cross-culturally effective and inspiring. And without an integrated eco-spirituality, the envisaged transformation is unlikely to be a fulfilling promise of hope and deeper meaning.

> 8. *Avoid military activities damaging to the environment. . . . Recognize that peace is the wholeness created by right relationships with oneself, other persons, other cultures, other life, Earth, and the larger whole of which all are a part. (6e; 16f)*

Russia's invasion of Ukraine in 2022 is a disturbing example of a superpower that does not operate out of a consciousness of "the larger whole of which all are a part."

The devastating damage to the environment illustrates all too clearly that violence to people and to nature is all of a piece. Correspondingly, as the ancient notion of Shalom indicates, peace is not merely the absence of violence or war but a conscious collaborative effort to work for those "right relationships" that enable all life to flourish and evolve. This is what Christians are asked to pursue in the name of the new reign of God (the new companionship). Just as the Jesus vision sought the demolition of every invasive empire, so in our world today we seek to bring about an end to all imperial power-mongering, striving to build a world of love and justice to the benefit of all sentient beings on earth.

A New Call to Conversion

In the Earth Charter there is no split between sacred and secular, and the multidisciplinary foundation that I propose for eco-spirituality today is also a central feature of the Charter. From both perspectives the vision is clear, and the mandate for the future calls for urgent and concerted action. Translating the vision into action, however, remains a formidable challenge for the human species today.

As already suggested, when humans began playing God, invoking power and domination over the natural world, we began to lose the plot. As we entered the agricultural era (some ten-thousand years ago), seeking domination and control over every aspect of nature, we began to dislodge what previously sustained a more organic way of being in the world. Today we are confronted with what Christians name a call to conversion, but the conversion involved in eco-spirituality is significantly different from that of formal religion.

The envisaged conversion requires us to revisit the exalted and exaggerated role of the human mind and tone down the inherited emphasis on rationality we so widely take for granted. The quality of analysis, objectification, and commodification holds our world to ransom, plummeting humanity along the slippery slope of the Anthropocene. We need to review the underlying assumptions and challenge the ensuing manipulation and exploitation.

Consider this strategy, proposed by American philosopher Charles Eisenstein, for a way forward:

> None of the problems facing humanity today are technically difficult to solve. Holistic farming methods could heal soil and water, sequester carbon, increase biodiversity, and actually increase yields to swiftly solve various ecological and humanitarian crises. Simply declaring a moratorium on fishing in half the world's oceans would heal them too. Systemic use of natural and alternative healing modalities could vastly reduce COVID mortality, and reverse the plagues of autoimmunity, allergies, and addiction. New economic arrangements could easily eradicate poverty. However, what all of these easy solutions have in common is that they require agreement among human beings. There is almost no limit to what a unified, coherent society can achieve. With coherency anything is possible. Without it, nothing is. (Eisenstein 2022, 85)

As a species with a sacred story of some seven million years, we have been through many major crises. More than survived, we have actually thrived and flourished.[8]

---

[8] This bold assertion will raise many eyebrows. With the emerging scientific wisdom of anthropological and paleontological research, we

The challenge now facing us, as eco-spiritual pioneers of our time, is to recapitulate the creative spirit of our deep story and mobilize it afresh to co-create a more empowering future for ourselves and for all earth's creatures. In this way we hope to contain the eco-anxiety that specialists claim is becoming an ever-increasing predicament for our time (Vakoch and Mickey 2022). I describe this challenge as *an invitation to homecoming*. The following are some of the key elements:

- Being at home in the cosmic creation is a precondition not merely for survival but for the articulation and development of our deeper selves.
- Being grounded in our earthiness is a precondition for feeling at home in creation as earthlings. Immersed more organically in our bioregions is what is at stake here.
- Close to the earth and its unfolding dynamics, we stand a better chance of befriending the many paradoxes within which creation flourishes.
- We need to come home to our bodies, love them authentically, and overcome the woundedness and abuse of so much disembodied rationality.

---

are surfacing a growing body of evidence to understand our previous major deviations, how we overcame major crises, and what we now have to learn to help us rework our current planetary dilemmas. Fortunately, thanks to much of the scientific wisdom of our time and the growing body of human intuitive wisdom, we can discern a change of direction that is likely to guarantee a more wholesome future. Graeber and Wengrow (2021) support this more optimistic view; however, their evidence is largely based on the hunter-gatherer phase of our evolution, dating back no more than fifty-thousand years ago.

- We need to abandon the religious theories of a fundamental flaw and reeducate ourselves on how to befriend in an informed and responsible way the recurring paradoxes within which creation flourishes.
- Our politics and economics have been sequestered by those addicted to patriarchal power, alienating rather than empowering the masses. A very different quality of political and economic engagement is necessary if we are to befriend creation in a more informed and responsible way.
- When we engage with all the above in a more enlightened way, we stand a better chance of living in a more godlike manner, not in subservience to a ruling sky-god, but in greater harmony with the Great Spirit, long known to our Indigenous Peoples.

This adventure is not a case of going back to some pristine previous existence, an idyllic past that never actually existed. Evolution never works in reverse. Moreover, internally, we know that creation always operates in terms of the paradoxical wisdom of birth-death-new life. We have been through the paradox many times. More intuitive people know it in their own bodies almost every day of their lives. Hopefully, we can come home to that which is more true and real and, in that way, bring about on earth the liberating hope acclaimed in the closing text of the Earth Charter:

Let ours be a time remembered for the awakening of a new reverence for life, the firm resolve to achieve sustainability, the quickening of the struggle for justice and peace, and the joyful celebration of life.

Critical Issues for Ongoing Discernment

1. Including the natural world in how we live our faith is not peripheral to Jesus and the Gospels but of central importance. The popular Greek-inspired dualistic split between sacred and secular does not belong to the vision and praxis of Jesus.

2. "Since the reign of God is especially attentive to the needy and outcast, Jesus showed a partisanship for suffering people that we can today interpret as extending to encompass the earth and its myriads of distressed species and ecosystems. His ministry reveals a wideness in God's mercy that includes all creation." (Johnson 2018, 82).

3. Prior to the time of Constantine's imperial rule (306–37), Christianity flourished in a highly flexible manner, with a transparency capable of embracing the earth-centered approach to faith outlined in the present work.

4. Throughout the Middle Ages, particularly between 1100 CE and 1300 CE, a mystical and eco-feminist spirituality flourished, offering precedents that challenge and inspire us in our present-day attempts to rehabilitate eco-spirituality.

5. The Earth Charter can serve us today as a blueprint for how we can translate eco-spirituality into daily practice for the sanctification and empowerment of person and planet alike.

The COP Climate Conferences and Eco-Spirituality

Unless there is a spiritual revolution that challenges the destructiveness of our technological genius, we will not save our planet.

—KAREN ARMSTRONG

In the 1990s, climate change emerged as a global problem often related to the burning of fossil fuels and the release of harmful gases by industries, resulting in a rise in global warming, with its negative impact on several aspects of planetary life. These include the melting of icecaps, rising sea waters, forest fires, and increasingly destructive storms. The ensuing damage is most noticeable among the world's poorest and most vulnerable peoples. Each year since 1995, the United Nations Framework Convention on Climate Change (UNFCCC) convenes an international gathering of key government delegates and climate activists, known as the Conference of the Parties (COP), to assess progress in dealing with the urgent challenges of climate change in our time. Since its launch, much of its work is focused on two critical issues: (1) The reduction of greenhouse gas emissions, in keeping with the Kyoto Protocol of the 1997

187

COP; and (2) the Paris Agreement of 2015, outlining international strategies to be adopted by all governments to reduce greenhouse gases to keep global temperature increase under 1.5 degrees centigrade, with the goal of achieving global net zero emissions by 2050.

All COP conferences since 1995 have highlighted the fact that the greatest offenders in these destructive climate patterns are the richer nations, including China, India, the United States, and several European countries. Only at the 2022 conference in Sharm el-Sheik, Egypt, did the world governments agree on a strategy to address the loss and damage caused to poorer nations by the rich and powerful.

The Enigma of Climate Change

The climate emergency has become a major contemporary challenge in which all global citizens are expected to take remedial action. According to the United Nations Environment Programme, "around two-thirds of global greenhouse gas emissions are linked to private households."[1] The electricity we use, the food we eat, the way we travel, and the things we buy all contribute to a person's "carbon footprint," the amount of greenhouse gas emissions associated with an individual's activities. Yet, the problem is primarily rooted within the large-scale realm of consumption-driven big business, corporation activity, and global trade practices. To use religious language, then, the primary call to conversion is

---

[1] Additionally, "the richest 1% of the global population account for more emissions than the poorest 50%." The online, interactive United Nations Environment Programme's "Emissions Gap Report 2020" contains useful information for all of us to know as we seek to live as better relatives with earth and one another.

for the world leaders in the political, economic, and commercial spheres.

We also encounter a highly complex picture when we review the role that weather patterns play in the evolution of life. Extreme weather patterns, more than anything else, are a primary impetus for evolutionary change. Without this paradoxical phenomenon, we would not have the rich complexity that constitutes universal life today. Consequently, the current wave of global warming is not merely a human phenomenon, nor is it caused primarily by irresponsible human behavior. Humans are certainly accelerating the destructive impact, and that requires substantial change in several features of our behavior. If, however, those changes are to make a difference for ourselves and for planetary life at large, they must also encompass the larger paradoxical reality of climate change as a force for both destruction and recreation. In this regard, a faith foundation as envisaged in eco-spirituality is of central importance.

The story of British climate activist Tamsin Omond helps to highlight the challenge facing us all:

I spent my twenties scared of climate disaster and busy organising. In my early thirties, I burnt out from living with zero balance and too much activism. When I realised that heaping it all on me wasn't just impossible but also delusional, I felt like I'd failed at the only thing that gave my life meaning. . . . We have pushed both our planet and ourselves, ignoring natural limits. Instead of learning from the earth about how to rest, heal and regenerate, we celebrate humankind as separate from and dominating nature. I want to let go of such an arrogant worldview. I want to give up trying to control the natural world and other humans

too. Fighting bad policies is part of a new story that
is taking root, but to heal we don't just need to fight,
we also need to become enchanted by the planet again.
(Omond 2021, 25)

That is precisely what this book is about: becoming enchanted
by creation once more. Eco-spirituality attempts to outline
the process of enchantment, along with various strategies to
focus afresh our spiritual and theological priorities.

Climate Emergency and COVID-19

As a human species, the call to become more responsible
regarding the climate emergency invites us to review several
other aspects of our behavior that are alien to the ecological
health of people and planet alike. The critical issue I wish
to highlight becomes all too apparent in how we dealt with
the COVID-19 crisis of 2019–2022. When the virus first
began to spread rapidly in the early part of 2020, several
world governments imposed lockdowns of various types.
This slowed down human movement, and we witnessed
clear, unpolluted skies, fishes returning to cleaner waters,
and natural habitats regaining something of their pristine
nature. Various voices across the world suggested that CO-
VID-19 felt like a wakeup call for the human species. Across
media channels commentators were referencing the need
for a "new normal."[2] At its annual gathering in June 2020,

---

[2] One of my favorite versions is that of Sonya Renee Taylor, which
reads in part: "We will not go back to normal. Normal never was.
Our pre-corona existence was not normal other than we normalized
greed, inequity, exhaustion, depletion, extraction, disconnection, con-
fusion, rage, hoarding, hate and lack. We should not long to return

and again in January 2021, the World Economic Forum called for a "new reset" in politics, economics, technology, and primarily the need for a major shift in consciousness (Schwab and Malleret 2020).

In December 2020, the first vaccines were rolled out, primarily across the rich nations of the West. From there on, we heard very little about the wakeup call, the new normal, or the need for a new reset. From the human perspective the vaccines were the magic (divine?) solution to the entire problem. And yes, the vaccines did benefit humans and saved millions of lives, but deeper and more urgent issues were left unaddressed, most serious of all, the actual cause of this global pandemic.

In September 2021, the Pasture Institute in Paris, France, confirmed that COVID-19 originated in the wet markets of Wuhan, China, as a result of the exploitative treatment that humans meted out to nonhuman creatures, in this case, bats. Prior to this announcement several scientists, notably Dan Quammen (2012) of the United States, had developed the theory of *zoonotic spillover*, noting that most, if not all, of the major viruses of the past fifty years arose from the exploitation and abuse of birds, mammals, or animals. COVID-19 was yet one more example of this sordid, commercial practice.

COVID-19 has continued to affect humans, with an ever-greater number of variants arising and vaccines having to be adapted to keep the virus at bay. And yet, virtually nobody is suggesting that we should shift the focus to the actual

---

my friends. We are being given the opportunity to stitch a new garment. One that fits all of humanity and nature" (Sonya Renee Taylor, Instagram, March 31, 2020).

causes and review afresh the reckless human behavior that caused the virus in the first place.

Let's return to the climate emergency and confront the daunting question facing our species today: *If we can't face the destructive reality of COVID-19, a global emergency that affected the entire human race, what hope do we stand against such a complex phenomenon as climate change?* In his opening address to the COP 27 gathering at Sharm el-Sheikh in Egypt, United Nations Secretary-General António Guterres confronted the delegates with a grimly disturbing picture reminiscent of the prophetic denunciation we encounter in the Hebrew scriptures: "We are on a highway to climate hell," he said, "with our foot still on the accelerator. Humanity has a choice: cooperate or perish. It is either a Climate Solidarity Pact—or a Collective Suicide Pact."

Being at Home on the Earth

If we humans can't listen to the painful anguish of the nonhuman beings who share the planet with us—forty-nine billion animals slaughtered in 2020 alone—I doubt if our species will pay much attention the apocalyptic rhetoric of António Guterres. We need to start closer to home. We need to come to terms with the fact that we too are earthlings, like the animals, mammals, birds, and fish. In his papal exhortation, *Beloved Amazonia*, issued on February 12, 2022, Pope Francis reminds us that, when we strip away the life-resources of the Amazonian forests, we are destroying some of the finest healing elements of organic life (Francis 2022). Most important of all, we need to relearn what it means to become bioregional persons, engaging the intimacy and immediacy of our earth for our nourishment, health, and general well-being—the "enchantment" highlighted by Omond (2021). We need a spirituality that will urge us on in this endeavor.

In terms of climate change and the targets set by previous COP conferences, I support the need for serious and substantive action, specifically the goal to restrict global temperature increase to 1.5 degrees centigrade. I also support what individuals and human communities are urged to do:

- Power our homes with renewable energy and use energy-saving appliances.
- Drive fuel-efficient vehicles and use public transport whenever possible.
- Reduce the carbon footprint arising from air travel; use electronic media for business and meetings.
- Consume food locally produced, thus reducing the energy spent on processing, packaging, and shipping.
- Reduce and recycle waste.
- Restore nature to absorb more carbon.
- Engage politicians and governments on the challenges of climate emergency.

It is difficult to gauge how much of an impact such behaviors will have, but at the very least they will help to change human consciousness in the direction of more sustainable and responsible ways of living upon this earth. However, all these suggestions are based on an assumption that humans, being creatures of elevated intelligence, can learn to treat the earth (as an object) differently.

Eco-spirituality requires a further move, one that is significantly greater. It requires us to outgrow and abandon our superior status and view the earth (and its resources) not as an object but as a lifeform that begets all other lifeforms, humanity included. Our human behavior needs to change in how we treat the earth and its resources, and in how we begin to identify with our earth as earthlings, creatures whose entire existence is begotten from and sustained by the living earth itself. Nothing short of such a substantial move is likely to alter the destructive impact we are currently exerting upon climate and other earthly life processes.

As indicated so often throughout this book, we need to start with a major shift in human identity as earth-centered creatures grounded more authentically in our bioregions. In that attempt to come home to where we truly belong, we can make a difference that will benefit all life, human and nonhuman alike.

Reference List

Abram, David. 2010. *Becoming Animal: An Earthly Cosmology*. New York: Vintage Books.

Albrecht, Glenn. 2019. *Earth Emotions: New Words for a New World*. Ithaca, NY: Cornell University Press.

Aquinas, Thomas. 1911-1925. *Summa theologica*. Translated by Fathers of the English Dominican Province. New York: Benziger Brothers.

——. 2010. *Summa Contra Gentiles*. Turnhout, Belgium: Brepols.

Armstrong, Karen. 1996. *In the Beginning*. London: Vintage.

——. 2019. *The Lost Art of Scripture*. London: Vintage Books.

——. 2022. *Sacred Nature*. London: The Bodley Head.

Asla, Reza. 2017. *God: A Human History of Religion*. New York: Penguin Books.

Baumeister, Dayna. 2014. *Biomimicry Resource Handbook: A Seed Bank of Best Practices*. North Charleston, SC: CreateSpace.

Bauman, Zygmunt. 2000. *Liquid Modernity*. Cambridge (UK) Polity Press.

Benedict XVI. 2010. "If You Want to Cultivate Peace, Protect Creation: Message of His Holiness Pope Benedict XVI for the Celebration of the World Day of Peace." January 1, 2010.

——. 2020. *Caritas in Veritate (Charity in Truth)*. June 20.

Benyus, Janine M. 1997. Reissued 2002. *Biomimicry: Innovation Inspired by Nature*. New York: HarperCollins.

Berry, Thomas. 1985. *The Dream of the Earth*. San Francisco: Sierra Club.

Boff, Leonardo. 1995. *Ecology and Liberation*. Maryknoll, NY: Orbis Books.

———. 2013. *Christianity in a Nutshell*. Maryknoll, NY: Orbis Books.

———. 2015. *Come Holy Spirit*. Maryknoll, NY: Orbis Books.

Bregman, Lucy. 2014. *The Ecology of Spirituality*. Waco, TX: Baylor University Press.

Bregman, Rutger. 2020. *Humankind: A Hopeful History*. New York: Bloomsbury.

Brisch, Nicole, ed. 2008. *Religion and Power*. Chicago: Oriental Institute of the University of Chicago.

Brock, Rita, and Rebecca Parker. 2008. *Saving Paradise*. Boston: Beacon Press.

Brown, Ronald J. 2018. "Religion and Technology in the Twenty-First Century." *Journal of Unification Studies* 19 (2018).

Brunet, M., et al. 2002. "A New Hominid from the Upper Miocene of Chad, Central Africa." *Nature* 418: 145-51.

Burdon, Peter, Klaus Bosselmann, and Kirsten Engel. 2019. *The Crisis of Global Ethics and the Future of Global Governance: Fulfilling the Promise of the Earth Charter*. Cheltenham, UK: Edward Elgar Publishing Ltd.

Cannato, Judy. 2006. *Radical Amazement*. Notre Dame, IN: Sorin Books.

Caputo, John D. 2015. *Hoping against Hope*. Minneapolis: Fortress Press.

Carroll, James. 2014. *Christ Actually*. New York: Viking.

Challenger, Melanie. 2021. *How to Be Animal*. Edinburgh: Canongate Books.

Chamorro-Premuzic, Tomas. 2023. *I, Human: Automation, and the Quest to Reclaim What Makes Us Unique*. Brighton, MA: Harvard Business Review Press.

Cheal, David. 1988. *The Gift Economy*. New York: Routledge.

Chittister, Joan. 1998. *Heart of Flesh*. Grand Rapids, MI: Eerdmans.

Choné, Aurélie, Isabelle Hajek, Philippe Hamman, eds. 2017. *Rethinking Nature: Challenging Disciplinary Boundaries*. New York: Routledge.

Christie, Douglas E. 2013. *The Blue Sapphire of the Mind*. New York: Oxford University Press.

Clegg, Brian. 2021. *The Patterns That Explain the Universe.* Cambridge, MA: MIT Press.

Collins, Christopher. 2013. *Paleopoetics: The Evolution of the Pre-literate Imagination.* New York: Columbia University Press.

Crosby, Michael. 2012. *Repair My House.* Maryknoll, NY: Orbis Books.

Crossan, John Dominic. 2010. *The Greatest Prayer.* New York: HarperCollins.

———. 2022. *Render unto Caesar.* New York: HarperCollins.

Currivan, Jude. 2017. *The Cosmic Hologram: In-formation at the Center of Creation.* Rochester, VT: Inner Traditions.

Dart, Raymond. 1925. "Australopithecus Africanus: The Man-Ape of South Africa." *Nature* 115: 195-99.

Dartnell, Lewis. 2019. *Origins: How the Earth Shaped Human History.* London: Vintage.

Davies, Paul. 1983. *God and the New Physics.* New York: Simon and Schuster.

Deacon. Terence. 1997. *The Symbolic Species.* New York: Penguin.

Deino, Alan, Paul R. Renne, Carl C. Swisher III. 1998. "40Ar/39Ar Dating in Paleoanthropology and Archeology." *Evolutionary Anthropology Issues News and Reviews.* 6: 63-75.

Delio. Ilia. 2011. *The Emergent Christ.* Maryknoll, NY: Orbis Books.

———. 2015. *Making All Things New: Catholicity, Cosmology, Consciousness.* Maryknoll, NY: Orbis Books.

———. 2021. *The Hours of the Universe: Reflections on God, Science, and the Human Journey.* Maryknoll, NY: Orbis Books.

Dennett, Daniel. 1991. *Consciousness Explained.* Boston: Little Brown.

Dürr, Hans-Peter. 2010. *Geist, Kosmos, und Physik.* Amerang (Germany): Crotona Verlag GmbH.

Dyer, Wayne. 2004. *The Power of Intention.* Carlsbad, CA: Hay House Inc.

d'Eaubonne, Françoise. 1974. *Le Féminisme ou la Mort.* Paris: Pierre Horay.

Earth Charter, The. 2001. Earth Charter Initiative. Available in fifty languages online.

Edinger, Edward F. 1984. *The Creation of Consciousness: Jung's Myth for Modern Man*. Toronto: Inner City Books.

Edwards, Denis. 2017. *Christian Understandings of Creation: The Historical Trajectory, Christian Understandings*. Minneapolis: Fortress Press.

Ehrman, Bart. 2018. *The Triumph of Christianity*. London: Oneworld Publications.

Einstein, Albert. 1936. "Physics and Reality." *The Journal of the Franklin Institute* 221: 349-82.

Eisenstein, Charles. 2011. *Sacred Economics*. Berkeley, CA: Evolver Editions.

———. 2022. *The Coronation*. White River Junction, VT: Chelsea Green Publishing.

Faber, Roland. 2004. *God as Poet of the World*. Louisville, KY: Westminster John Knox Press.

Farley, Wendy. 2011. *Gathering Those Driven Away: A Theology of Incarnation*. Louisville, KY: Westminster John Knox Press.

Fox, Everett. 1983. *The Five Books of Moses*. New York: Schocken.

Fox, Matthew. 1983. *Original Blessing*. Santa Fe, NM: Bear and Co.

———. 2011. *Christian Mystics*. Novato, CA: New World Library.

———. 2014. *Meister Eckhart*. Novato, CA: New World Library.

———. 2020. *The Tao of Thomas Aquinas*. Bloomington, IN: iUniverse Publications.

Francis. 2015. *Laudato Si': On Care for Our Common Home*. Vatican City: Libreria Editrice Vaticana.

———. 2020. *Fratelli tutti*. October.

———. 2022. *Querida Amazonia*. Vatican City: Libreria Editrice Vaticana.

Frazer, James George. 1894. *The Golden Bough: A Study in Comparative Religion*. 2 vols. New York: MacMillan and Co.

Fuentes, Agustin. 2017. *The Creative Spark*. New York: Dutton.

Goff, Philip. 2019. *Galileo's Error: Foundations for a New Science of Consciousness*. London: Rider/Penguin.

Gowlett, J.A.J. 1984. *Ascent to Civilization*. New York: McGraw-Hill.

———. 2011. "The Vital Sense of Proportion." *Paleoanthropology*. 2011: 174-187.

Graeber, David, and David Wengrow. 2021. *The Dawn of Everything*. London: Allen Lane.

Grey, Mary. 2006. "From Shaken Foundations to a Different Integrity: Spirituality as a Response to Fragmentation." *Concilium*, 79-87.

Haight, Roger. 2019. *Faith and Evolution*. Maryknoll, NY: Orbis Books. Harman, Jay. 2014. *The Shark's Paintbrush: Biomimicry and How Nature Is Inspiring Innovation*. Ashland, OR: White Cloud Press.

Haught, John F. 2010. *Making Sense of Evolution*. Louisville, KY: Westminster/John Knox Press.

———. 2015. *Resting on the Future*. New York: Bloomsbury.

Herzfeld, Noreen. 2009. *Technology and Religion: Remaining Human in a Co-created World*. West Conshohocken, PA: Templeton Press.

Heying, Heather, and Bret Weinstein. 2021. *A Hunter Gatherer's Guide to the Twenty-First Century*. New York: Random House.

Horan, Daniel P. 2019. *Catholicity and Emerging Personhood*. Maryknoll, NY: Orbis Books.

Howard-Brook, Wes. 2016: *Empire Baptized: How the Church Embraced What Jesus Rejected*. Maryknoll, NY: Orbis Books.

Hyland, Richard. 2009. *Gifts: A Study in Comparative Law*. New York: Oxford University Press.

John Paul II. 1999. "Respect for Human Rights: The Secret of True Peace: Message of His Holiness Pope John Paul II for the Celebration of the World Day of Peace." January 1, 1999.

Johnson, Elizabeth. 1993. *Women, Earth, and Creator Spirit*. New York: Paulist Press.

———. 2007. *Quest for the Living God*. New York: Continuum.

———. 2014. *Ask the Beasts! Darwin and the God of Love*. New York: Bloomsbury.

———. 2018. *Creation and the Cross*. Maryknoll, NY: Orbis Books.

Kaku, Michio. 2019. *The Future of Humanity*. New York: Doubleday.

Keller, Catherine. 2003. *Face of the Deep*. New York: Routledge.

Kim, Grace Ji-Sun. 2011. *The Holy Spirt, Chi, and the Other*. New York: Palgrave Macmillan.

Kraybill, Donald B. 1990. *The Upside Down Kingdom*. Scottdale, PA: Herald Press.

Kurzweil, Ray. 2005. *The Singularity Is Near*. New York: Viking.

Lanzetta, Beverly. 2018. *The Monk Within*. Sebastopol, CA: Blue Sapphire Books.

Lee, Dora. 2011. *Biomimicry: Inventions Inspired by Nature*. Toronto: Kids Can Press.

Lent, Jeremy. 2017. *The Patterning Instinct*. Lanham, MD: Prometheus Books.

———. 2021. *The Web of Meaning*. Gabriola Island, Canada: New Society Publishers.

Levi-Strauss, Claude. 1978. *Myth and Meaning*. London: Routledge and Kegan Paul.

Levy, Paul. 2018. *The Quantum Revelation: A Radical Synthesis of Science and Spirituality*. New York: SelectBooks.

Lewis-Williams, David. 2002. *The Mind in the Cave*. London: Thames and Hudson.

MacGregor, Neil. 2018. *Living with the Gods*. London: Penguin Books.

Malone, Mary. 2014. *The Elephant in the Church*. Dublin: Columba Press.

McGinn, Bernard. 1991. *The Foundations of Mysticism*. New York: Crossroad.

McIntosh, Christopher. 2004. *Gardens of the Gods: Myth, Magic, and Meaning*. London: I. B. Taurus.

Meier, John P. 1994. *A Marginal Jew: Rethinking the Historical Jesus, Voume 2, Mentor, Message, and Miracles*. New Haven, CT: Yale University Press.

Merton, Thomas. 1961. *New Seeds of Contemplation*. New York: New Directions.

Mickey, Sam. 2020. "Spiritual Ecology: On the Way to Ecological Existentialism." *Religions* 11 (11): 580.

Mitsch, William J., and Sven Eric Jorgensen. 2004. *Ecological Engineering and Ecosystem Restoration*. Hoboken, NJ: Wiley.

Moltmann, Jürgen. 1985. *God in Creation: A New Theology of Creation and the Spirit of God*. San Francisco: Harper and Row.

Naess, Arne. 1976. *Ecology, Community and Lifestyle: Outline of an Ecosophy*. Cambridge, UK: Cambridge University Press.

Neusner, Jacob. 2014. *What Is Midrash?* Eugene, OR: Wipf and Stock.

Oakley, Kenneth. 1949. *Man the Tool-Maker*. London: British Museum.

Omond, Tamsin. 2021. *Do Earth: Healing Strategies for Humankind*. London: The Do Book Company.

O'Murchu, Diarmuid. 2008. *Ancestral Grace*. Maryknoll, NY: Orbis Books.

———. 2011. *In the Beginning Was the Spirit*. Maryknoll, NY: Orbis Books.

———. 2014. *On Being a Postcolonial Christian*. North Charleston, SC: CreateSpace.

———. 2017. *Incarnation: A New Evolutionary Threshold*. Maryknoll, NY: Orbis Books.

———. 2018. *Beyond Original Sin*. Maryknoll, NY: Orbis Books.

———. 2019. *When the Disciple Comes of Age*. Maryknoll, NY: Orbis Books.

———. 2021. *Doing Theology in an Evolutionary Way*. Maryknoll, NY: Orbis Books.

———. 2022. *Paschal Paradox: Reflections on a Life of Spiritual Evolution*. Cincinnati, OH: Franciscan Media.

Ord, Toby. 2020. *The Precipice: Existential Risk and the Future of Humanity*. New York: Bloomsbury.

Orr, Emma Restall. 2012. *The Wakeful World: Animism, Mind, and the Self.* Alresford, UK: Moon Books.

Osiek, Carolyn, and Margaret MacDonald. 2007. *A Woman's Place.* Minneapolis: Fortress Press.

Pannenberg, Wolfhart. 1972. "Doctrine of the Spirit and the Task of a Theology of Nature." *Theology* 75: 8–21.

Papagianni, D., and M. A. Morse. 2013. *Neanderthals Rediscovered.* London: Thames and Hudson.

Phipps, Carter. 2012. Evolutionaries. New York: Harper Perennial.

Quammen, David. 2012. *Spillover: Animal Infections and the Next Human Pandemic.* New York: W. W. Norton.

Rambo, Shelly. 2010. *Spirit and Trauma.* Louisville, KY: Westminster John Knox Press.

Renfrew, Colin. 2009. *The Sapient Mind: Archaeology Meets Neuroscience.* New York: Oxford University Press.

Rifkin, Jeremy. 2009. *The Empathic Civilization.* Cambridge (UK): Polity Press.

Rohr, Richard. 2019. *The Universal Christ.* New York: Convergent Books.

Rohr, Richard, and J. Patrick Boland. 2021. *Everything Is Sacred.* New York: Convergent Books.

Ruether, Rosemary Radford. 1983. *Sexism and God Talk.* London: SCM Press.

Russell, Stuart. 2019. *Human Compatible: Artificial Intelligence and the Problem of Control.* New York: Viking.

Rynne, Terrence J. 2008. *Gandhi and Jesus: The Saving Power of Nonviolence.* Maryknoll, NY: Orbis Books.

Sagan, Carl. 1994. *Pale Blue Dot: A Vision of the Human Future in Space.* New York: Random House.

Satlow, Michael, ed. 2013. *The Gift in Antiquity.* Malden, MA: Wiley.

Schwab, Klaus, and Thierry Malleret. 2020. *Covid-19: The Great Reset.* Geneva, Switzerland: FORUM Publishing.

Schwager, Raymund. 1987. *Must There Be Scapegoats? Violence and Redemption in the Bible.* New York: HarperCollins.

Service, Steven R. 2015. *The Lost and Forgotten Gospel of the Kingdom*. Morrisville, NC: Lulu.com.

Sheldrake, Merlin. 2020. *Entangled Life*. London: The Bodley Head.

Spong, John Shelby. 2016. *Biblical Literalism: A Gentile Heresy*. New York: HarperOne.

Sprinkle, Preston. 2021. *Nonviolence: The Revolutionary Way of Jesus*. Colorado Springs, CO: David C. Cook. Previously published in 2013 as *Fight: A Christian Case for Nonviolence*.

Stavrakopoulou, Francesca. 2021. *God: An Anatomy*. London: Picador.

Stout, Dietrich. 2016. "Tales of a Stone Age Neuroscientist." *Scientific American* (Special Edition) 25: 28-35.

Swanson, Jennifer. 2020. *Beastly Bionics*. Washington, DC: National Geographic Partners.

Taylor, John. 1972. *The Go-Between God*. London: SCM Press.

Taylor, Steve. 2005. *The Fall*. Winchester (UK): O Books.

Teilhard de Chardin, Pierre. 1969. *Human Energy*, trans. J. M. Cohen. New York: Harcounrt Brace Jovanovich.

Tetlow, Joseph A. 1995. *An Ecological Spirituality*. Washington, DC: United States Conference of Catholic Bishops.

Tonelli, Guido. 2021. *Genesis: The Story of How Everything Began*. London: Profile Books.

Torrance, Thomas F. 1972. "Newton, Einstein, and Scientific Theology." *Religious Studies* 8: 233-50.

Tucker, Mary Evelyn, John Grim, and Willis Jenkins. 2017. *Routledge Handbook of Religion and Ecology*. New York: Routledge.

Vakoch, Douglas A., and Sam Mickey. 2022. *Eco-Anxiety and Pandemic Distress*. New York: Oxford University Press.

Vearncombe, Erin, Bernard Brandon Scott, Hal Taussig, and Sue Monk Kidd. 2022. *After Jesus, Before Christianity*. New York: HarperOne.

Vondey, Wolfgang. 2009. "The Holy Spirit and the Physical Universe." *Theological Studies* 70: 3-36.

Von Essen, Carl. 2010. *Eco-Mysticism*. Rochester, VT: Bear and Co.

Wallace, Marc I. 2018. *When God Was a Bird*. New York: Fordham University Press.

Weber, Andreas. 2014. *Matter and Desire: An Erotic Ecology*. White River Junction, VT: Chelsea Green Publishing.

———. 2016. *The Wonder of Biology*. Gabriola Is., BC: New Society Publishers.

Willoughby, Pamela R. 2005. "Palaeoanthropology and the Evolutionary Place of Humans in Nature." *International Journal of Comparative Psychology* 18: 60-91.

Wink, Walter. 2003. *Jesus and Nonviolence*. Minneapolis: Fortress Press.

Winter, Miriam Therese. 2009. *Paradoxology*. Maryknoll, NY: Orbis Books.

Wirzba, Norman. 2019. *Food and Faith*. New York: Cambridge University Press.

———. 2022. *Agrarian Spirit*. South Bend, IN: Notre Dame University Press.

Woodburn, James. 1970. *Hunters and Gatherers: The Material Culture of the Nomadic Hadza*. London: British Museum.

Yong, Ed. 2016. *I Contain Multitudes*. London: Vintage.

Index

Milton Keynes UK
Ingram Content Group UK Ltd.
UKHW022152100924
448154UK00012B/234

9 781626 985698